EXPORT DYNAMICS AND ECONOMIC GROWTH IN LATIN AMERICA

Export Dynamics and Economic Growth in Latin America

A comparative perspective

SHEILA AMIN GUTIÉRREZ DE PIÑERES
University of Texas at Dallas

MICHAEL J. FERRANTINO
United States International Trade Commission

Routledge
Taylor & Francis Group
LONDON AND NEW YORK

First published 2000 by Ashgate Publishing

Reissued 2018 by Routledge
2 Park Square, Milton Park, Abingdon, Oxon OX14 4RN
711 Third Avenue, New York, NY 10017, USA

Routledge is an imprint of the Taylor & Francis Group, an informa business

A Library of Congress record exists under LC control number: 00130119

ISBN 13: 978-1-138-70432-9 (hbk)
ISBN 13: 978-1-315-20276-1 (ebk)

Contents

List of Figures

List of Tables

Prologue

Furthermore, my child, you must realize that writing books involves endless hard work, and that much study wearies the body. - *Ecclesiastes 12:12.*

This book began with a discussion on the campus of Southern Methodist University in late 1992, when one of the coauthors was teaching there and the other was in residence at the University of Arkansas in Fayetteville. One of us had done very little work on the Latin American economies, being primarily absorbed in microeconometric work related to India. The other was a macroeconomic theorist, motivated by recent developments in Latin America but just beginning the transition to empirical work. In general, theorists and empiricists ought to collaborate more often; at least this is what normative views of progress in science tell us ought to happen. Anyway, it seemed like a good idea at the time. It is for the reader to judge whether this particular collaboration has yielded fruitful insights or not.

At first, we had no notion that we were writing a book. The canons of professional advancement for economists indicate that research should be released in discrete chunks the size of journal articles, and books are supposed to be for senior economists. After working on export diversification and growth in Latin America for awhile, though, it became apparent that the whole might be greater than the sum of the parts, and that a synthetic, cross-country perspective would help us to draw out the implications of our research agenda. After much helpful support and encouragement from Dr. Brian Berry, we decided to expand upon our previous work into its present form.

A previous version of the material in Chapter Two appeared in *Latin American Business Review*, forthcoming; of Chapter Three, in *The International Executive*, Vol. 39, no. 4 (July/August), pp. 465-477; of Chapter Four, in *Journal of Development Economics*, Vol. 52, no. 2 (April), pp. 375-391, and of Chapter Five, in *Review of Development Economics,* vol.3, no. 3, (October) pp.268-280; of Chapter Eight, in *Singapore Economic Review*, vol. 41, no. 1 (April), pp. 13-24. Sebastian Edwards, E. Kwan Choi, Denise Dimon, and Yahia Zoubir provided us with helpful editorial comments at the time of first publication, and we benefitted from the comments of a number of anonymous referees. Chapters One, Six, Seven, and Nine represent new material for this volume. We have made some minor corrections to the original published material, such as updating references to working papers which have since become accessible as published articles. As will be apparent, our thinking on the central questions of the research agenda has evolved over time. In the case of material previously published elsewhere, we have let our original statements stand rather than attempt to enforce an arbitrary consistency.

We are particularly grateful to Grant Gardner, mutual friend and colleague, for performing the requisite introductions and inadvertently giving birth to this research agenda. We are greatly indebted to our most formative teachers in the economics of international trade and economic development, particularly to Robert Evenson, T.N. Srinivasan and Carlos Díaz-Alejandro for Michael and Kent Kimbrough, Anne O. Krueger, Philip Brock, and Robert Bates for Sheila. Sheila would also like to acknowledge Dr. Steve Pejovich, who continually encourages her to reach for new challenges, and to honor the memory of G. Douglas Jenkins, whose advice she recalls often in her pursuit to be a scholar and academic. Conference participants at the following annual conferences, during 1992-1998, American Economics Association Meetings held in conjunction with the Allied Social Sciences Association, Southern Economic Association, and Business Association for Latin American Studies and at the U.S. International Trade Commission for helpful comments. Special thanks to Joseph Ziegler, economics department head at the University of Arkansas, who was very supportive of this not so mainstream line of research and never complained about the high phone bills and travel costs associated with this line of research. We also would like to thank the College of Business at the University of Arkansas for a small international grant that allowed us to hire Joyce Roberts to input data. Also certain data for Colombia was collected while Sheila was on a Fulbright Senior Research/Lecture Grant in Colombia in 1994. The invaluable editorial support of the staff, particularly Mrs. Claire Annals, at Ashgate Publishing Limited throughout all stages of the process has been greatly appreciated. Able research assistance was provided by Nurlan Turdaliev and Rodolfo Hernandez. Also to the participants of POEC 6376: Policy Research Workshop: Latin American Policy Analysis, at The University of Texas at Dallas, who worked on individual country projects and updated the data files. A special thanks to Inske Zandvliet (and Dr. Euel Elliott for assigning her time to me) for all her invaluable assistance in the preparation of the manuscript and the index. A final thanks must go to Sheila's parents for their support (including countless hours of babysitting) while we were rushing to meet deadlines.

In particular, we are grateful for the support of Victor Gutiérrez de Piñeres and Karen Burrell. Their encouragement and good humor (Victor's, while Sheila was writing and computing in Dallas, and Karen's, while Michael was doing the same in Fredericksburg) have sustained us throughout the process of being first-time authors. This book is dedicated to them, our spouses.

As is always the case, any deficiency in the present volume is not to be attributed to any of the above persons, but solely to the authors themselves. In particular, it should be noted that the views expressed in this book are those of the authors, and none of the views expressed herein are meant to represent the views of the U.S. International Trade Commission, any of its individual Commissioners, or indeed of any of our current or former employers.

1 Introduction

The New Latin Trade Boom

The last decade has seen renewed interest in international trade as a possible engine of growth for Latin America. The export pessimism of many Latin American economists in the immediate postwar period, which provided intellectual arguments in support of the inward-looking policies of most of the region's governments, has been replaced by a boom both in trade itself and in policy moves to further liberalize trade. The present volume represents an attempt to revisit a long-standing issue, the relationship between export diversification and economic growth in Latin America, in the light of new empirical evidence and in a way which may shed some light on the current debates regarding trade policy in Latin America.

This boom is manifest in several ways. Latin American exports have recently grown rapidly by a number of measures, each of which provides a different perspective on the current situation. First, Latin American economies have become more open in general, in terms of the share of GDP accounted for by trade. Latin American exports as a share of GDP have risen from a trough value of less than 8.7 percent as recently in 1972 to nearly 14 percent in 1996, with half of this rise taking place during the last five years (Figure 1.1). This mirrors the general pattern by which trade growth has exceeded output growth worldwide over the long run; the corresponding ratios for the world are about 10.2 percent in 1972 and 18.9 percent in 1996. As many economists have noted, the global tendency for trade growth to exceed output growth has persisted for at least the last fifty years, and arguably for the last 250 years (Easterlin, 1996, p.40), so by the simplest crude measure of increasing outward orientation Latin America is not particularly unusual.

Second, during the 1990s Latin American exports have grown twice as rapidly as world exports, at 11.17 percent per annum as opposed to 5.6 percent per annum (Table 1.1). This performance has reversed a long-run trend under which the growth of Latin American exports lag behind that of world exports, mirrored by the rapid rise of exports in other regions such as East Asia. Consequently, the share of Latin American exports in world exports has risen sharply, from a trough of 3.58 percent in 1991 to 4.58 percent in 1996 (Figure

1.2). This recovery in the global share of Latin America's exports has reversed the previous slump only modestly; Latin American exports exceeded 8 percent of the global total as recently as 1963.

Third, in the last decade, the most rapidly recent growing component of Latin American trade has been intra-Latin trade. Intra-Latin exports have grown from 12.5 percent of total Latin American exports in 1985, to 15.8 percent in 1990, to 20.4 percent in 1995 (derived from Statistics Canada, *World Trade Analyzer* database). This growth, rapid as it has been, represents an emergence from an immediate post-debt crisis trough, and the current level of intra-Latin exports, either as a share of total Latin American exports or of world exports, is comparable with levels frequently observed in the last 50 years; as recently as 1980 intra-Latin exports accounted for 22.4 percent of total Latin American exports.

There are three types of explanations generally offered for the secular tendency of trade to grow more rapidly than income; declining transport and communications costs, trade liberalization, and the possibly above-average income elasticity of traded goods (on this last, see Pogany and Donnelly, 1998). In the Latin American case, many observers have attributed the increase in trade in general, and in intra-Latin trade in particular, to recent moves towards trade liberalization in the region. First, most Latin American countries moved to reduce tariffs sharply following the debt crisis of the early 1980s. Dean, Desai and Riedel (1994), p.96, characterize the pre-reform average nominal tariff to be 'about 44 percent...by the early 1990s, these tariff levels had fallen by 65 percent...', implying an average tariff *circa* 1992 of around 15 percent for all of Latin America. The extent of individual tariff cuts for a number of Latin American countries are summarized in Table 1.2.

Second, trade integration within the Western Hemisphere has been promoted through a series of regional integration schemes, which have proliferated in complexity (Organization of American States, 1997; Inter-American Development Bank 1998). In 1991, Argentina, Brazil, Paraguay, and Uruguay signed the Treaty of Asunción, establishing MERCOSUR (Common Market of the Southern Cone: abbreviated as MERCOSUL in Portuguese), providing for phased-in tariff elimination on most products among the members, and implementing a common external tariff on most products in January 1, 1995. Also in 1991, negotiations commenced among Canada, Mexico, and the United States, leading to implementation of NAFTA (North American Free Trade Agreement) on January 1, 1994. NAFTA imposed immediate tariff elimination on a large number of goods, with others facing phaseouts of five, ten or (in a few cases) fifteen years. The Group of

Three agreement among Colombia, Mexico, and Venezuela, entering into force in 1995, provides for phased tariff reductions on most products over a 10-year period. The Andean Group, Central American Common Market, and CARICOM (Common Market of the Caribbean Community), established during the 1960s and 1970s, were reinvigorated in the 1990s with new internal liberalizations and (in the case of the Andean Group) a new common external tariff. In addition, the 1990s have seen numerous bilateral liberalization agreements in the hemisphere, mostly initiated by Chile and Mexico.

Table 1.1 Annual Growth of Real Exports

	Latin America	World
1963-70	3.16	7.50
1970-75	12.55	15.31
1975-80	10.80	10.77
1980-85	-13.83	-5.43
1985-90	3.37	9.51
1990-96	11.17	5.76

Source: World Bank, *World Development Data 1998*. Nominal dollar figures deflated for using the U.S. GDP deflator.

All of these initiatives are ultimately scheduled to be folded into the new FTAA (Free Trade Association of the Americas), unveiled at the Miami summit of December 1994, with the goal of completing a free trade zone for the entire Western Hemisphere, excluding for the moment Cuba, by December 31, 2004. Negotiations for the FTAA, which began in earnest in May 1998, encompass a diversity of 'deep integration' issues in addition to the traditional concerns of tariffs and quantitative restrictions taken up by the negotiating groups on market access. Additional negotiating groups deal with investment, services, dispute settlement, government procurement, agriculture, competition policy, and the combined area of subsidies, anti-dumping and countervailing duties. For its part, the Council of Ministers of LAIA (Latin American Integration Association), successor to the old LAFTA (Latin American Free Trade Association), approved a series of rules for its members permitting partial waivers of MFN obligations as well as a scheme of compensation negotiations to ease the potential international legal conflicts induced by the unfolding of the current spaghetti-like network of new trade initiatives.

Old and New Thinking on Export Diversification, Trade, and Growth

The debate about whether export diversification is important for economic growth has persisted from the beginning of modern development economics, as has the related debate about whether economic growth is more likely to be experienced by exporters of some products (e.g. manufactures) than other products (e.g. primary products). While there has not at any point been a strong consensus, economists born after 1960 are generally less familiar with the passions the topic once aroused. Hla Myint (1964) summarized the state of the argument as of 1964:

> Some of the orthodox economists were inclined to assume too readily that the expansion of international trade would automatically transmit economic growth to the underdeveloped countries, and the 'specialization' in the production of those primary products most suited to their resources would automatically raise their general level of skills and productivity and lead to a more productive combination of resources. Nowadays, the pendulum has swung to the opposite extreme, not only among the political leaders of the developing countries but among professional economists also. It is now generally assumed that the expansion of primary exports is highly unlikely ever to provide a satisfactory basis of continuous economic growth for the underdeveloped countries (p. 27).

The standard arguments for the gains from trade through specialization, whether of the Ricardian or the Heckscher-Ohlin variety, provide no ground for supposing that having a wide variety of exportables is particularly conducive to national welfare. England ought to export cloth, and Portugal wine, on the grounds of comparative advantage. Even in the multi product extensions of classical and neoclassical trade theory, in which each country exports many products and the theory's job is to identify the product with the marginal capital-labor ratio, it may be that in the market equilibrium one country exports N products while the other country exports $M < N$ products, but for the second country to try to diversify further by exporting $M+1$ products would involve nothing more than a welfare-destroying distortion.

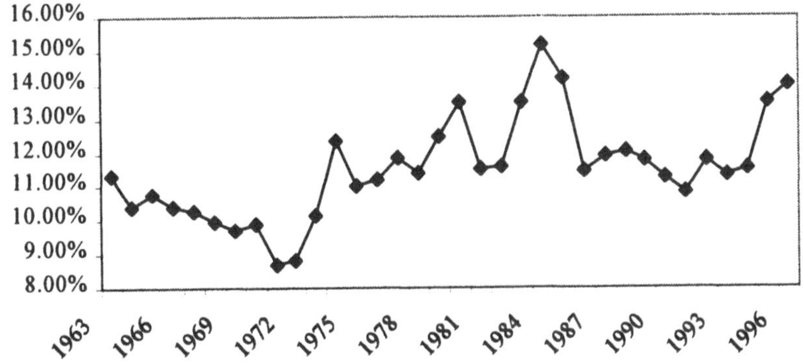

Figure 1.1 Latin American Exports as a Share of Latin American GDP

Bhagwati (1966, 5), in pressing the neoclassical case, went as far as to claim that there is no empirical relationship between per capita income and either the degree of export diversification or the variance of export revenues. Arguing from scatter plots and tables (not a particularly low-tech way to proceed in those days of expensive regression), he stated that the tendency for exports to be concentrated among three principal commodities bore no significant negative relationship to per capita GDP, and that an index of export earnings instability was also unrelated to per capita GDP. It is unclear that the first conclusion would stand up under more careful analysis of Bhagwati's data; of his sample of 62 countries, 9 of the 31 most-diversified are classified as 'non-underdeveloped' (and the sample includes the United States), while only 3 of the 31 least-diversified are so classified (and one of these is Venezuela). The critique of the relationship between export earnings stability and income is probably stronger. Even so, on the facts available at the time, Bhagwati (1964) conceded that 'for most underdeveloped countries: 1 instability in export earnings is fairly high; and 2 these earnings come largely from a few primary commodities ... Instability poses problems of domestic and international adjustment which few economic administrations in the underdeveloped countries are either trained or equipped to solve. A nation that concentrates on a limited range of primary exports faces the risk that the markets for them may have limited prospects of expansion'(p. 61).

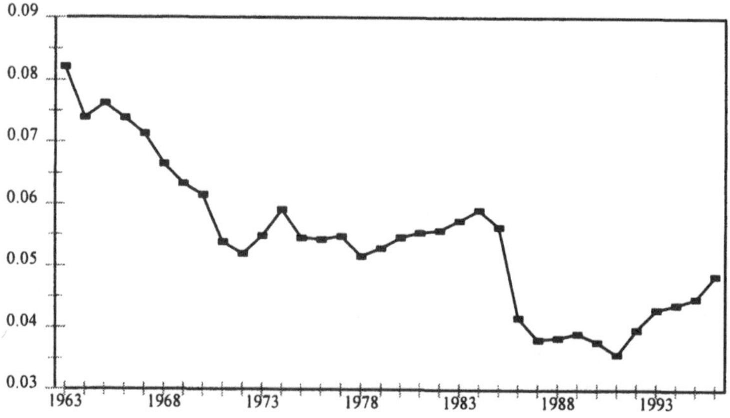

Figure 1.2 Latin American Exports as a Share of World Exports

The argument in favor of export diversification on the grounds that diversifying the export portfolio reduces export earnings stability is probably the most widely accepted, as it is independent of either a neoclassical, structuralist, or dependency-school perspective *per se*. The difficulties that non-diversified developing countries may face with price and revenue instability of exports have been appreciated at least since Keynes (1938). If one assumes that income instability is more costly to the poor (which can follow either from a moral argument or from the declining marginal utility of income), and that export earnings instability leads to income instability, then diversification is particularly valuable to poorer countries. Alternately, if capital accumulation is essential for growth, that countries in early stages of development must import a high share of capital equipment, then it follows that stable export earnings are necessary for stable capital accumulation and thus economic growth. Downturns in export earnings are then particularly costly, because a poor country's already small capital stock will suffer depreciation due to the inability to import replacement equipment or spare parts.

Diversification may be useful in reducing export instability, but it is costly in two ways (Myint, 1964, pp.148-9). First, as in any portfolio choice, there is a tradeoff between high-risk/high-income and low-risk/ low-income portfolios. A country whose production is fully specialized according to its comparative advantage will maximize its income in the neoclassical way, but that income is subject to the variance of revenue induced by price fluctuations in the product of specialization. Producing a diversity of products reduces variance of income but sacrifices some of the gains of specialization. Moreover, it may be difficult for developing countries to shift smoothly from one product mix to another as world prices change due to inadequate development of internal labor and capital markets. This suggests that diversification is an easier strategy to pursue for developed than developing countries, on institutional grounds alone.

The structuralist arguments of Raul Prebisch (1950) and Hans Singer (1950, 1987), lying outside the neoclassical tradition, argued that exporters of primary products are systematically disadvantaged over the long run. The widely familiar Prebisch/Singer argument is of particular interest for our story, not only because a case for export diversification away from primary products and towards manufactures can easily be made from it, but because, through the UN's Economic Commission for Latin America (CEPAL, in Spanish), these arguments provided influential intellectual support for the actual policies of import substitution that most Latin countries followed in the postwar period, and are still popular in certain academic and political circles in the region. It is in large part due to Prebisch and Singer that many economists, even some of neoclassical orientation, automatically identify diversification with a shift from 'traditional' primary products to 'non-traditional' manufactures, a view we challenge in this book.

Prebisch and Singer argued that there is a general trend toward declining terms-of-trade for primary products. Four reasons were giving for this: (1) Primary commodities were thought to be relatively price-inelastic, so that increases in revenues were not readily obtained through price cuts. (2) Primary commodities were thought to be relatively income-inelastic (a generalization of Engel's Law for food, although many primary commodities are nonfood (oil, copper, cotton) or luxury foods (sugar, cocoa). (3) Technological innovation and market power in Northern manufactured goods meant that the prices of these goods embody both a Schumpeterian rent element for innovation and a pure monopoly rent. (4) Both product and labor markets in industrial countries were more oligopolistic, raising the relative price of manufactured good. Independently of what happens to the terms of trade, it

Table 1.2 Average Tariffs in Latin America

Country	Pre-Reform	Post-Reform	1995
MERCOSUR			
Argentina	42(1987)	15(1991)	13.9
Brazil	51(1987)	21(1992)	12.7
Paraguay	NA	16(1991)	9.5
Uruguay	32(1987)	18(1992)	9.6
ANDEAN			
Bolivia	12(1985)	8(1991)	9.7
Colombia	61(1984)	12(1992)	11.4
Ecuador	37(1989)	18(1992)	11.2
Peru	NA	17(1992)	16.3
Venezuela	37(1989)	19(1991)	11.8
CACM			
Costa Rica	61(1984)	12(1992)	10.2
El Salvador	NA	NA	10.2
Guatemala	50(1985)	15(1992)	10.2
Honduras	41(1985)	15(1992)	10.1
Nicaragua	NA	NA	10.1
CARICOM			
Antigua and Barbuda	NA	NA	14.1
Barbados	NA	NA	14.1
Belize	NA	NA	14.3
Dominica	NA	NA	13.9
Grenada	NA	NA	14.1
Guyana	NA	NA	15.0
Jamaica	NA	20(1990)	14.0
St. Kitts and Nevis	NA	NA	13.9
St. Lucia	NA	NA	13.9

Table 1.2 Continued

Country	Pre-Reform	Post-Reform	1995
St. Vincent and Grenadines	NA	NA	13.7
Suriname	NA	NA	14.0
Trinidad and Tobago	NA	41(1991)	14.1
OTHER			
Chile	35(1984)	11(1991)	11.0
Mexico	24(1985)	13(1990)	14.0

Note to Table 2: Columns I and II are from A. Alam and S. Rajapatirana, 'Trade Reform in Latin America and the Caribbean', Finance and Development, September 1993, and represent average unweighted legal tariff rates. Column III is from the Inter-American Development Bank Applied Tariffs Data Bank and gives the MFN applied rate, p.96 , characterize the pre-reform average nominal tariff to be 'about 44 percent. . .by the early 1990s, these tariff levels had fallen by 65 percent. . .', implying an average tariff c. 1992 of around 15 percent for all of Latin America.

has been argued that many primary products may have limited (income-inelastic) demand, or on the supply side, their production may be subject to diminishing returns. These would provide further reasons for trying to diversify into the export of manufactures.

Empirically, the claim of declining net barter terms of trade for primary products has been widely questioned since the empirical work of Spraos (1980). Subsequent empirical research has not supported the hypothesis of a general declining trend in the terms of trade for developing countries (Grilli and Yang, 1988). In addition, while certain export commodities have had have highly volatile price swings, the price index of the overall primary commodity basket of Latin American exports has not been particularly volatile (Lord and Boye, 1991). More broadly, many authors have noted that it is possible to achieve high levels of income while maintaining a significant primary-product specialization in international trade. The United States, Canada, Australia, New Zealand, and Denmark are all developed countries with important net exports in agriculture, while Kuwait, Saudi Arabia, and the United Arab Emirates maintain relatively high levels of income with an almost exclusive specialization on petroleum. Thus, there is nothing automatic about the linkage between an export specialization in manufactures and high living standards.

Regardless of what one thinks of the intellectual merit of the Prebisch/Singer arguments, they have had practical consequencesfor countries which have acted on them by pursuing policies of import substitution. Import substitution, by inducing production in a wider variety of products than market forces would have otherwise brought about, can lead to export diversification *as measured quantitatively* by the analyst. The roots of this process can be seen in the idea of a deliberate 'balanced-growth' program of industrialization (Rosenstein-Rodan, 1943), which, while not necessarily identical to a program of import substitution, is intellectually akin to it. The 'big push' of a balanced-growth program was to consist of industrialization in many sectors simultaneously, in a pattern consistent with rising domestic consumer demands. Though not initially directed at export (Rosenstein-Rodan visualized the countries in question exporting agricultural goods and importing capital equipment, and so excluded these sectors from the 'big push') it is easy to imagine how a country attempting to industrialize on a balanced-growth basis could find either that some factories in some industries had achieved export-level degrees of efficiency, or (more likely) that subsidies to manufacturing introduced as part of the 'big push' would drive output prices in some sectors down to the point that they would find themselves exporting. (Of course, on the neoclassical view, simultaneous industrialization to achieve balanced growth is unnecessary, since imbalances between domestic supply and demand can be accommodated through international trade).

Outside of Latin America, India provides a good case in point (Bhagwati and Srinivasan, 1975; Wolf, 1982). Various export promotion measures were introduced in the 1960s, including direct cash assistance, import replenishment licenses, drawback of excise and import duties, subsidized credit, freight and income tax concessions, and export processing zones. During the 1960s and 1970s, growth rates of Indian exports such as machinery and transport equipment and chemicals far exceeded growth rates either of primary products or of manufactures made of such products as jute, leather, and cotton. These growth rates proved unsustainable in later years. In our own work, we find that something similar happened in Latin America, as heavy industrial goods are 'traditional' exports in more than one country.

The empirical finding of large volumes of intraindustry trade between developed countries in similar, but slightly differentiated products (Balassa,

1966; Grubel and Lloyd, 1975) gave rise to the so-called 'new international trade theory' (Krugman, 1979; Dixit and Norman, 1980, 9; Helpman, 1981; Ethier, 1982). In these models, economies of scale and product differentiation give rise to trade in differentiated products of the type observed in the data. Since differentiated-productstrade is associated with developed countries, and traditional Heckscher-Ohlin trade is associated with developing countries (as in, e.g. Markusen, 1986), students of these theories may well receive a vague impression that export diversification is associated with affluence in general. However, to our knowledge the new trade theory has not generally placed great focus on what the dynamic transition from being a Heckscher-Ohlin exporter to a Helpman-Krugman exporter might look like, nor on what the likely results of such a transition would be for living standards.

The theme of a multiplicity of products also permeates many of the newer theories of endogenous growth. These models often utilize concepts of increasing returns to scale and product differentiation similar to those in the new trade theories. Alternately, or at the same time, they may invoke processes of technical innovation, diffusion, and externalities associated with these to obtain their results. There have been a number of attempts to link the newer growth theories to international trade. Two accessible presentations are in Grossman and Helpman (1991), Chapters Nine to Twelve, Barro and Sala-I-Martin (1995), Chapter Eight. These models contain a large and ever-increasing number of products due to innovation, with new products being constantly innovated in the developed 'North' and being imitated in the developing 'South'. For a certain range of equilibria, more rapid Southern imitation may lead to both a greater variety of Southern exports and larger aggregate volume of Southern exports, as well as higher welfare, suggesting that successful export diversification at least *can* be desirable. Nonetheless, the new trade-growth models generally yield ambiguous results on such basic questions as whether trade liberalization itself is welfare-improving at all. Answers to such secondary questions as the growth or welfare effects of export diversification are then in turn ambiguous *a priori*, leaving the question for empirical analysis.

Amin Gutiérrez de Piñeres (1996) provides an endogenous growth model in which increased exports are unambiguously associated with higher growth rates. In this model, the reallocation of human capital from the import-competing sector to the export sector generates positive technological externalities, which in turn induce growth. One motivation for this idea is that technological or marketing knowledge which has proven successful in one line of exporting can easily diffuse into other lines of exporting. For example, the export success of Chilean table grapes demonstrated the feasibility of other exports of Chilean fresh fruit, and Colombian exports of fresh cut flowers were followed by other highly perishable produce. While the model does not contain an explicit measure of export diversification, the motivation for the existence of externalities attributed to the export sector is consistent with the idea of a felicitous nexus among export diversification, technical diffusion, and economic growth.

Indeed, the observation that relatively 'low-tech' exports of developing countries can be readily stimulated by diffusion of even very basic technological improvements is of long standing. Myint (1964, pp. 38-42) contrasted the expansion of 'plantation exports' such as coffee or rubber with that of 'peasant exports' such as rice, cocoa, palm oil or cotton. In countries such as Burma, Thailand, Ghana, Nigeria, and Uganda, rapid expansion of peasant exports was stimulated by basic improvements in transport and communications in remoter districts, which facilitated both improved marketing and the rule of law. Foreign export-import firms were introduced to act as middlemen between the peasants and the world market. Thus, diffusion of relatively simple improvements in infrastructure and institutions can stimulate primary-product exporting, with increased exports leading to further innovations in these areas, perpetuating a virtuous cycle.

The implications of such a process for broader growth and trade policy are fascinating:

> (P)easant export production expanded without the introduction of radical improvements in the agricultural techniques used in subsistence production, and that when the peasants took to 'specializing' in export crops it merely meant that they were devoting the whole of their resources to export production. In doing this they took full advantage of the *market opportunities* available to them; but this does not mean that they took full advantage of the *technical opportunities* to improve their productivity ... Two very different policy conclusions can be drawn from this. The first is that peasant export expansion is not likely to be a satisfactory basis for a continuous and self-sustained type of economic development, and that therefore these countries should turn to manufacturing industry. This is the conclusion favoured by many of the newly independent developing countries in South-East Asia and Africa...Thus, they tend to divert the larger part of the proceeds from peasant exports obtained through the marketing boards and other forms of taxation to industrial development, so starving the peasant sector of capital and technical assistance. But an entirely different conclusion can be drawn. ... opportunities for improvement (in production

> techniques) have been neglected ... it will be necessary for (these economies) to raise productivity in peasant production if only to release the labour required for their industrialization (Myint ,1964, p. 52; emphasis in original).

While at the time of Myint's writing Latin America appeared to have relatively little in the way of 'peasant exports', the more recent experience in Chile, Colombia, and elsewhere indicates that the process of agricultural export stimulated by accumulated experience of small-scale producers with increased access to basic means of productivity enhancementis well underway, and is contributing significantly to Latin American growth.

The Latin American Experience

The idea that Latin American exports can be stimulated by a 'grass-roots' process of innovation and learning, which would in turn transform the commodity composition of exports, has not been much emphasized for most of the history of Latin American export policy. As recently as 1976, Celso Furtado could write:

> In studying the long-term trends of the Latin American economies, perhaps the single most striking feature is the immutability of the region's export pattern ... the region's capacity to import is still dependent on exports of a few primary products, which were already being exported before 1929 ... in the period 1948 to 1970, Latin American exports grew at a rate less than half that of the increase in the total value of world trade. The region's participation in world trade, which was 11 percent in 1948, fell to 7 percent in 1960 and 5 percent in 1970 (Furtado, 1976, p. 209).

The idea that without government intervention, Latin American countries would be locked into an eternal reliance on a historically-given set of export commodities, and that this would be bad on Prebisch/Singer - type arguments, has stimulated a range of interventionist policies to modify the composition of trade. Latin American countries have historically taken a number of steps to regulate and control their export sectors, most notably by means of managing the price of a principal export commodity. Mexico nationalized foreign oil companies in 1938, leading to the establishment of PEMEX, one of the largest companies in Latin America, public or private. Special export taxation on oil began in Venezuela in 1944, with rates steadily increasing in order to provide a greater share of profits to the government, and finally nationalization of a 50 percent share in the industry in 1948. In Brazil, an export tax on coffee, introduced in 1906, was used to finance the purchase of coffee surpluses for the purpose of price stabilization. In 1961, Brazilians established GERCA (the Executive Group for the Rationalization of Coffee Growing), which organized the uprooting of 1.4 billion coffee trees, and in the following year persuaded other producers and consumers to establish the International Coffee Organisation, with the intent of regulating worldwide marketing of coffee. Argentina established an elaborate system of multiple exchange rates in the 1930s, and took control of export prices from 1946 to 1955 through the Institute for the Promotion of Foreign Trade (IAPI). Government intervention in the Chilean copper industry began in 1951, with an agreement placing 20 percent of foreign firms' output at the disposal of the central bank, expanded through the 'Chileanization' policy of state majority ownership in the mid-1960s, and culminated in the nationalization of Anaconda Copper in 1969 and of other foreign corporations after the 1971 constitutional changes of Salvador Allende's Unidad Popular government (Furtado, Ch. 17).

At the same time, many Latin American countries pursued policies of import-substituting industrialization (See Cardoso and Helwege, 1992, Ch. 4, for a discussion.) From the 1930s through the 1980s, governments used a variety of measures such as overvalued exchange rates, import licensing, tariffs, direct government investment in heavy industries (sometimes with foreign partners), targeted credit subsidies, and subsidies on intermediate goods used by heavy industries, such as steel and electricity. The results of these efforts were mixed, with some enterprises relatively efficient by world standards but many requiring unsustainably increasing levels of state subsidy. In at least some cases, industries fostered by policies of import substitution generated exports, either by virtue of actual efficiency or as a result of subsidized low domestic prices. Both by directly exporting from state-encouraged manufacturing sectors and by withdrawing resources from primary-product sectors, import-substituting industrialization was capable of generating at least some export diversification as measured, and the rhetoric of import-substitutingindustrialization was consistent with the idea that export diversification was good, or at least that primary-product specialization was bad.

The Plan of the Book

Each of the succeeding six chapters takes up an aspect of the relationship between export diversification and economic growth in Latin America from the standpoint of empirical analysis. Chapters Two and Three lay out the broad stylized facts with respect to export diversification in international comparison. Chapters Four through Six present a series of country case studies of the diversification-growth relationship, for Chile, Colombia, and (as a contrasting pair) the oil exporters Mexico and Venezuela. Chapter Seven presents a cross-country econometric analysis of the diversification-growth relationship. Chapter Eight synthesizes some of the relationships between diversification, trade liberalization and growth in an analytical model, while Chapter Nine concludes with some observations about policy.

Chapter Two establishes that there has been a long-run trend toward export diversification in Latin America, which has persisted through both inward- and outward-looking policy experiments, and over a variety of macroeconomic conditions. Looking at a sample of six large economies (Argentina, Brazil, Chile, Colombia, Mexico, and Venezuela), structural change in exports accelerated during the debt crisis episode of the early 1980s, and more rapid structural change may have been associated with policy reform. The increase in export diversification implies that important sources of economic risk in Latin America may be declining over the long run. Importantly, the persistent secular nature of the diversification suggests that diversification is induced endogenously, by micro-level processes, rather than engineered.

In Chapter Three, we construct measures of export similarity among seventeen Latin American countries over a thirty-year period, and using cluster analysis, we analyze patterns of similarity or complementarity in the commodity composition of various countries' export portfolios. While exports of primary products have declined in importance for Latin America, they still play a significantly large role. There is a long-run trend towards increasing export similarity among Latin American countries, which consists of convergence between clusters and divergence within clusters. The potential for trade of differentiated, but broadly similar, manufactures has increased among Argentina, Brazil, and Mexico, but not for intra-Latin bilateral trade involving smaller countries. In an appendix to the chapter, our measure of export similarity generated is incorporated into an econometric model of bilateral aggregate trade in Latin America. The data reject a significant role for specialization of resource endowments (Heckscher-Ohlin trade) in explaining the historical development of intra-Latin trade. Intra-Latin trade is positively associated with scarcity of foreign exchange.

Chapter Four documents that in the case of Chile, a prolonged and extensive episode of export diversification and accelerated economic growth in Chile began in the mid-1970s and may still be ongoing. This episode coincides in timing with pronounced policy shifts in the direction of internal and external liberalization. Structural change in Chilean exports has historically accelerated during periods of internal crisis and external shock. This suggests that repeated exposure of a national economy to crises and shocks will induce diversification whether or not government policy deliberately aims at diversification.

Colombia (Chapter Five) is a country for which analysts have had particular difficulty finding evidence of 'export-led growth'. For both Colombia and Chile, this difficulty has been partially due to the emphasis the literature has placed on the econometric technique of Granger causality, and different insights can be obtained after export diversification and export structural change have been directly measured. Increases in the rate of export structural change are associated with accelerated Colombian GDP growth, while export diversification has not historically been a source of economic growth for Colombia. The association of export structural change with high growth in Colombia, but with low growth in Chile, indicates that there is no single standard mechanism by which diversification is related to growth in medium-run periods of several years in length.

The contrasting experiences of Mexico and Venezuela with oil revenues (Chapter Six) illustrate the ways in which national policies may simultaneously interact with export diversification and growth. Of all Latin American countries, Venezuela shows the greatest degree of reliance on a single export commodity, oil, and has historically shown the weakest tendency towards diversification. Historically high levels of oil income have reduced the perceived urgency of policy reform. The importance of oil in Mexico has been episodic, expanding markedly after the discoveries of the 1970s but being superseded in the 1980s and 1990s by a diverse array of manufactures, many of which have emerged because of conscious policy decisions favoring both general economic liberalization and economic integration with the United States. In the case of Mexico increasing export diversification supported economic growth.

In Chapter Seven, we revisit the relationship between export diversification, export structural change and growth in Latin America using standard cross-country growth empirics on panel data. We find a positive relationship between export diversification and economic growth of an economically important magnitude. There is no clear-cut relationship between export structural change and economic growth. Comparisons among the empirical features of growth in Latin America, sub-Saharan Africa and developing Asia indicate that these results are not likely driven by peculiarities of Latin American growth relative to other developing regions, since the determinants of Latin American growth are broadly similar to those of developing countries as a whole. We do find evidence that Latin America enjoys comparatively high rates of return to both domestic investment and foreign direct investment, and, consistent with this, that income convergence between poorer and richer countries in Latin America is relatively rapid.

Chapter Eight presents an analytical model in the endogenous-growth style which captures some of the possible dynamics of non-traditional export expansion in Latin America, motivated by such sectoral success stories as Colombian cut flowers and Chilean fruit. Human capital, a resource associated with both innovation and externalities, can be allocated into a country's exportable sectors or its import-competing sectors. Human capital invested in one export sector generates positive spillovers to the other exportable sectors, but not to the import-competing sector. This provides a mechanism by which trade liberalization is associated both with more rapid economic growth and with export diversification.

In Chapter Nine, we draw out some of the implications of the empirical research for the prospects of further Latin American integration. Intuitively, it may be argued that the prospects for the success of trade agreements depend on the scope for trading complementary products, and that given the continuing importance of traditional primary products in Latin America, the scope for complementarity is weak. After all, limited gains can be had from trading bananas for bananas, coffee for coffee, or even coffee for bananas. In the light of the empirical analysis, we can see that an appropriate set of stylized facts includes a long-run trend toward export diversification for most countries, increasing trade of differentiated manufactures among the largest countries, the historical unimportance of complementarity in explaining intra-Latin trade flows, the experience that more diversified Latin American countries have *ceteris paribus* grown more rapidly, and the relatively rapid convergence of Latin American incomes across countries. These facts, taken together, suggest that intra-Latin trade in the future is likely to increasingly resemble the trade in differentiated products observed among the wealthier developed countries. The expansion of such trade is consistent with the achievement of higher levels of economic development. Estimates of the gains from, say, MERCOSUR or the FTAA which are predicated on Heckscher-Ohlin specialization only are likely to be understated. Nonetheless, the ongoing role of the most traditional Latin exports in financing the capital accumulation necessary to sustain this growth is likely to persist.

References

Amin Gutiérrez de Piñeres, Sheila (1996), 'Externalities in the Export Sector and Long-Run Growth Rates', *Singapore Economic Review*, vol. 41 no. 1 (April), pp. 13-24.

Balassa, Bela (1966), 'Tariff Reductions and Trade in Manufactures', *American Economic Review* vol. 56, pp. 466-473.

Barro, Robert J. and Xavier Sala-I-Martin (1995), *Economic Growth*, New York: McGraw-Hill.

Bhagwati, Jagdish (1966), *The Economics of Underdeveloped Countries*, New York: McGraw-Hill.

Bhagwati, Jagdish and T.N. Srinivasan (1975), *Foreign Trade Regimes and Economic Development: India* (New York and London: Columbia University Press for the National Bureau of Economic Research).

Cardoso, Eliana and Ann Helwege (1992), *Latin America's Economy: Diversity, Trends, and Conflicts*, Cambridge, MA: MIT Press.

Dean, Judith, Seema Desai and James Riedel (1994), 'Trade Policy Reform in Developing Countries Since 1985: A Review of the Evidence', *World Bank Discussion Paper* 267, Washington, DC: World Bank.

Dixit, Avinash, and Victor D. Norman (1980), *Theory of International Trade*, Cambridge: Cambridge University Press.

Easterlin, Richard A. (1996), *Growth Triumphant: The Twenty-First Century in Historical Perspective*, Ann Arbor: University of Michigan Press.

Ethier, Wilfred (1982), 'National and International Returns to Scale in the Modern Theory of International Trade', *American Economic Review*, vol. 72 (June), pp. 950-959.

Furtado, Celso (1976), *Economic Development of Latin America: Historical Background and Contemporary Problems*, 2nd edition, Cambridge: Cambridge University Press.

Grilli, E. And C. Yang (1988), 'Primary Commodity Prices, Manufactured Goods Prices, and Terms of Trade of Developing Countries: What the Long Run Shows', *World Bank Economic Review*, vol. 2, no. 1.

Grossman, Gene M. and Elhanan Helpman (1991), *Innovation and Growth in the Global Economy*, Cambridge, MA: MIT Press.

Grubel, Herbert G. and Peter Lloyd (1975), *Intra-Industry Trade: The Theory and Measurement of International Trade in Differentiated Products*, New York: John Wiley.

Helpman, Elhanan (1981), 'International Trade in the Presence of Product Differentiation, Economies of Scale, and Monopolistic Competition: A Chamberlin-Heckscher-Ohlin Approach', *Journal of International Economics*, vol. 11 (August), pp. 305-340.

Inter-American Development Bank (1998), *Integration and Trade in the Americas*, Department of Integration and Regional Programs; Division of Integration, Trade, and

Hemispheric Analysis; Statistics and Quantitative Analysis Unit, Periodic Note (August). Washington, DC: IADB.

Lord, Montague and Greta Boye (1991), 'The Determinants of International Trade in Latin America's Commodity Exports', in Miguel Urrutia, ed., *Long-Term Trends in Latin American Economic Development*, Baltimore: John Hopkins University Press for the Inter-American Development Bank.

Keynes, John Maynard (1938), 'The Policy of Government Storage of Foodstuffs and Raw Materials', *Economic Journal*, vol. 48, September, pp. 449-60.

Krugman, Paul (1979), 'Increasing Returns, Monopolistic Competition, and International Trade', *Journal of International Economics*, vol. 9, pp. 469-479.

Markusen, James (1986), 'Explaining the Volume of Trade: An Eclectic Approach', *American Economic Review*, vol. 76, No. 5 (December), pp. 1002-1011.

Myint, Hla (1964), *The Economics of the Developing Countries*, New York: Praeger.

Organization of American States (1997), *Trade and Integration Agreements in the Americas: An Analytical Compendium*, Washington, DC: OAS.

Pogany, Peter and William A. Donnelly (1998), 'The Income Elasticity of Trade: Theory, Evidence and Implications', *U.S. International Trade Commission Office of Economics Working Paper* 98-09-A (September 3), Washington, DC: USITC.

Prebisch, Raul (1950), *The Economic Development of Latin America and its Principal Problems*, New York: U.N. Economic Commission on Latin America.

Rosenstein-Rodan, Paul N. (1943), 'Problems of Industrialization of Eastern and South-Eastern Europe', *Economic Journal*, 1943.

Singer, Hans W. (1950), 'The Distribution of Gains Between Investing and Borrowing Countries', *American Economic Review*, vol. 40 (May), pp. 473-85.

Singer, Hans W. (1987), 'Terms of Trade and Economic Development', in *The New Palgrave: A Dictionary of Economics*, John Eatwell, Murray Milgate and Peter Newman, Eds., London: The Macmillan Press.

Wolf, Martin (1982) *India's Exports*, New York: Oxford University Press for the World Bank, 1982.

2 Export Diversification Trends*

Introduction

The performance of Latin American exports in recent years has given rise to a resurgence of optimism in the region. According to the IMF *Direction of Trade* data, from 1980 through 1991, world exports grew at 6.1 percent per annum in nominal terms while export growth in Latin America ('Developing Western Hemisphere') lagged at 3.3 percent per annum. By contrast, from 1991 to 1994 Latin American export growth at 7.8 percent per annum outpaced world growth at 4.6 percent. The timing of this export growth in particular countries is closely associated with trade regime reform (Alam and Rajapatirana, 1993). Meanwhile, a proliferation of liberalization initiatives, including NAFTA, MERCOSUR, CARICOM, and numerous other regional and bilateral initiatives, has led policy makers to focus on the goal of completing a comprehensive scheme of Western Hemisphere trade integration by 2005 (Rivera, 1995), with Mexico and Chile testing the waters of Pacific Rim liberalization in APEC.

This renewal of export optimism contrasts sharply with an earlier, widely held view that immersion in international trade could hinder Latin American development by inducing a 'primary product trap'. Countries exporting such products as coffee, copper, beef or bananas were bound to fare poorly in international markets either because of a secular decline in the prices of primary products (e.g. Prebisch, 1950), because of 'unequal exchange' between primary products and manufactures (e.g. Amin, 1977), or because lack of diversification would expose 'single-export' countries to excessive volatility in the terms of trade, with associated negative effects on investment confidence (Helleiner, 1986). Consequently, schemes of import-substituting industrialization were advocated.

The present chapter is an attempt to establish some stylized facts about the process of export diversification and structural change in exports for six key

---

* This chapter printed with some revisions by the authors Amin Gutiérrez de Piñeres, Sheila and Michael J. Ferrantino, 'Export Diversification Trends: Some Comparisons for Latin America', *International Executive,* July/August 1997, vol. 39, no. 4, pp. 465-477.

Latin American economies: Argentina, Brazil, Chile, Colombia, Mexico and Venezuela. Our results show that there has been a long-run trend toward export diversification in the region which has persisted through both inward- and outward-looking policy experiments, and over a variety of macroeconomic conditions. Structural change in exports accelerated during the debt crisis episode of the early 1980s, and more rapid structural change may be associated with policy reform. In addition, there are important differences among regions in the pattern of export diversification.

Historical Overview

Latin America has a long tradition of economic liberalism dating back to the 19th century, punctuated by periodic experiments with import substitution. Maddison (1991), using data for 1913, illustrates that Latin America was much more integrated into the world economy than were the Asian countries. During this time period there was a great deal of foreign investment and growth rates were relatively high in Latin American countries. Additionally, 'the role of the state in the economy was relatively small, and the bureaucratic apparatus weak. The dominant ideology espoused democracy and laissez-faire' (Urrutia, 1991). Trade during this era was predominately with the developed world. Intra-Latin trade was minimal (Maddison, 1991).

The change in philosophy came after the world depression of 1929. Trade, migration, and capital restrictions forced Latin American countries to look inward for solutions. The volume of trade fell, as did world prices for Latin American exports (Maddison, 1991). The openness of Latin American economies magnified the effect of the U.S. depression on those economies. At this point, Latin America began to diverge from liberalism to a more inward-looking policy approach. Protectionist policies in Latin America continued during the post-World War II years, with largely satisfactory performance in terms of aggregate growth. As Maddison (1991) notes, 'Despite supply shortages, the countries had been able to grow successfully and to achieve rather easy import substitution without a large switch of resources to capital formation or any massive effort at universal training....'. Thus, while the rest of the world was moving back towards liberalism in the postwar period, Latin America saw no reason to diverge away from its policies of import substitution.

An intellectual rationale for inward-looking policies was provided by Raul Prebisch's hypothesis of export pessimism (1959). Prebisch, then president of the United Nations Economic Commission for Latin America and the Caribbean (ECLAC), expressed doubts about the ability of trade to be an engine of growth and saw declining terms of trade for primary products as hindering the growth of developing countries. Prebisch contended that price instability and declining terms of trade created a primary commodity export dependence that was the cause of slow growth. Subsequent empirical research has not supported the hypothesis of a general declining trend in the terms of trade for developing countries (Grilli and Yang, 1988). In addition, while certain export commodities have had have highly volatile price swings, the price index of the overall primary commodity basket of Latin American exports has not been particularly volatile (Lord and Boye, 1991).

In the 1960s, some effort was made to expand intra-Latin exports of manufactures through the creation of regional trading blocs such as LAFTA (Latin American Free Trade Association), the Andean Pact, and CACM (Central American Common Market). Given the similarity in resource endowments, these trading agreements only met with limited success (Maddison, 1991; Michaely, 1994). It was not until the second oil shock of 1979 and the debt crisis of the early 1980s that Latin American economies experienced significant pressure for trade liberalization, induced by the sharp economic contractions of the period. Sachs and Warner (1995), using their openness index, rank all six countries in this study as open after 1991, with Chile being classified as open as of 1976 and Colombia and Mexico as of 1986.

Simultaneously, individual countries have sought independently to promote their exports. Many countries created export promotion agencies (PROEXPO in Colombia, PROCHILE in Chile, SECOFI in Mexico, and PROMEXPORT in Venezuela) whose sole purpose was to expand export markets and encourage diversification in exports. There has always been a recognition of the 'desirability of diversifying exports away from primary commodities' (Urrutia, 1991). The initial push of these agencies was to expand exports of manufactured goods which proved to be a failure as these countries were not able to compete in world markets. Years of import substitution had created inefficient high cost industries which had been shielded from any real competition.

While overall policy has shifted from one of liberalism in pre WWI years to a more inward looking policy and, more recently, to trade liberalization, long-run trends have tended toward export diversification regardless of the policy stance. The following empirical analysis documents this point for the most recent epoch, beginning in the early 1960s.

Patterns of Diversification

Data on merchandise exports at the two-digit SITC level were collected for the period 1962-1993 (1962-1991 for Chile and Colombia) and deflated using appropriate commodity-specific deflators. For each year and country, an export specialization index was generated as follows:

$$SPECL_t = \sum_{i=1}^{54} (s_{i,t})^2$$

where $s_{it} = e_{it}/\Sigma_{i\in(1,54)}e_{it}$, the share of commodity I's exports in national exports in year t. SPECL thus takes on values approaching 1 if the country's exports are concentrated in a single commodity classification and values approaching 0 as exports become diversified.

The results of this exercise appear as Figures 2.1 and 2.2. Chile, Brazil and Colombia show secular trends in the direction of export diversification throughout the period. The trend in Chile is pronounced, and follows with a brief lag the Allende/Pinochet policy transition from socialism and nationalization to *laissez faire*. Mexico and Colombia also show secular trends toward diversification after accounting for the interruptionsassociated with the Mexican oil boom (c. 1978-1983) and the Colombian coffee boom (c. 1978-1985). Argentina remains at a high level of diversification throughout the period. The exception to the rule is Venezuela. The trend toward diversification in Venezuela is much weaker as oil has continued to dominate their exports.

The mean over the six countries of the specialization index is also presented in Figure 2.3, reinforcing the result that the trend toward export diversification in Latin America is indeed a long-run phenomenon.

A relatively constant aggregate level of diversification may mask a substantial degree of structural transformation in a country's comparative advantage, if different product groups are replacing each other in rapid succession. In order to capture this possibility we calculated an index of medium-run structural transformation in the following manner. As a first step, we calculated a cumulative export experience function for each commodity. This is obtained as:

$$c_{it} = \frac{\sum_{i\,t_0}^{t} e_{it}}{\sum_{i\,t_0}^{t_1} e_{it}}$$

where t_0 and t_1 represent the initial and terminal periods of the sample. The variable c_{it} has properties similar to that of a cumulative distribution function; it takes on values at or near 0 at the beginning of the sample period and rises to 1 in the final year. The cumulative export experience function was calculated for each commodity and country over all seven-year intervals; i.e. over 1962-1968, 1963-1969, etc., through 1987-1993.

The means of cumulative export experience for each commodity were then constructed as

$$T_i = \frac{\sum_{t\,t_0}^{t_1} c_{it}}{t_1 - t_0 + 1}$$

Commodities for which exports were concentrated earlier in the time period have a higher score for T_i. We refer to T_i as the 'traditionality index' since it can be used as an empirical measure of traditionality of exports when evaluated over a sufficiently long time period. Finally, a measure of medium-run structural change in exports, TRAD7, was calculated as the variance of the traditionality index calculated within countries and across commodities, centered on the median year. The value of TRAD7 for 1965, e.g. is the variance of the commodity values of T_i for a single country obtained using the period 1962-1968 as a reference period. When the variance is high, this implies a high degree of medium-run structural change in export composition.

Values of TRAD7 for the six economies are presented in Table 2.1, along with means. The period from 1977-1984 experienced the greatest degree of structural transformation, with means of TRAD7 across the six countries exceeding .024 in those years while falling below that threshold before and after. The mean of the TRAD7 index is also presented graphically in Figure 2.4. This result can potentially be explained in two ways. First, it may reflect a response to the debt crisis, as countries urgently seeking export revenue reallocated resources toward their comparative advantages (the debt transition years of 1980-1981 figure in the calculations of TRAD7 throughout 1977-1984). Alternatively, the mean may be driven by the single-commodity booms in Mexico and Colombia which happen to coincide with the debt crisis transition.

Inspection of the results country-by-country reveal some acceleration in medium-run structural transformation for each of the six countries over the relevant period, with some variations in timing. This suggests that the overall acceleration in structural transformation of exports was indeed related to the debt crisis. In addition, it can be demonstrated that at least for Chile, other episodes of structural transformation are associated with adverse shocks in macroeconomic conditions (Amin Gutiérrez de Piñeres and Ferrantino,1997).

Finally, the commodity structure of export transformation in each country was explored by calculating the traditionality index T_i for each commodity and country over the full sample period 1962-1993 (or 1962-1991 for Chile and Colombia). Table 2.2 presents the results of this exercise for the top ten two-digit SITC categories in each country. Again, a higher traditionality score implies that exports in that commodity were calculated earlier in the sample period, with scores exceeding .5 associated with secular declines in real exports. Lower traditionality scores are associated with more rapid growth in real exports in more recent years.

For Chile and Argentina, successful diversification has meant moving from a single primary product (copper, or beef) to a broader-based comparative advantage, with a particular emphasis in Chile on 'non-traditional' agriculture. Brazil and Mexico have followed a progression from primary to manufactured goods of the type often assumed to be normative for the process of development. Colombia has combined a Chilean-type agricultural broadening with an Asian-type deepening in the textile-apparel complex. Venezuela appears to be stuck in an oil-based primary product trap, while oil appears to have been a progressive influence in Mexico.

Conclusion

Investors often make much of political risk in the Latin American context. Our principal finding is that a principal source of *economic* risk for these economies, namely excessive export specialization, has tended to steadily decline even though political regimes and economic policies have frequently shifted. Increasing export diversification enhances the prospects of exchange

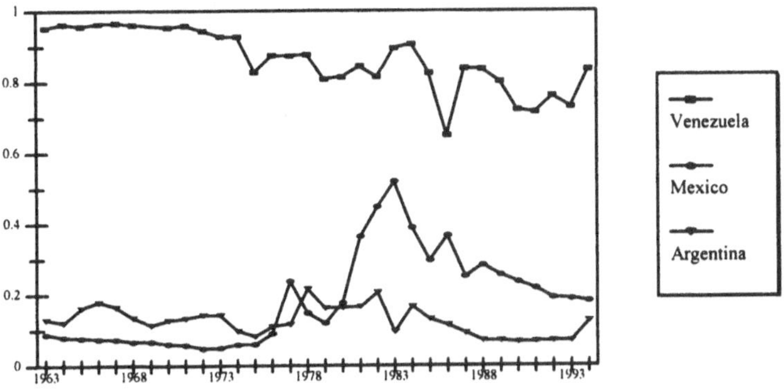

Figure 2.1 Specialization Index: 1963-1993

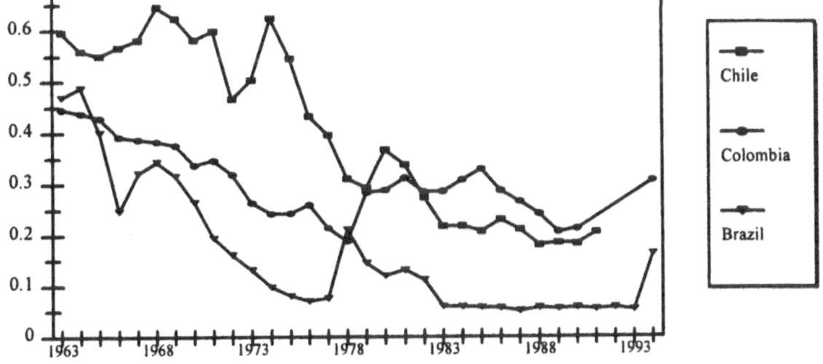

Figure 2.2 Specialization Index: 1963-1993

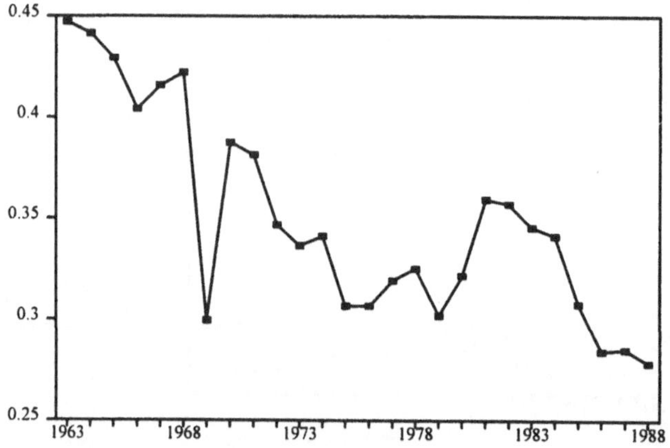

Figure 2.3 Mean Specialization Index

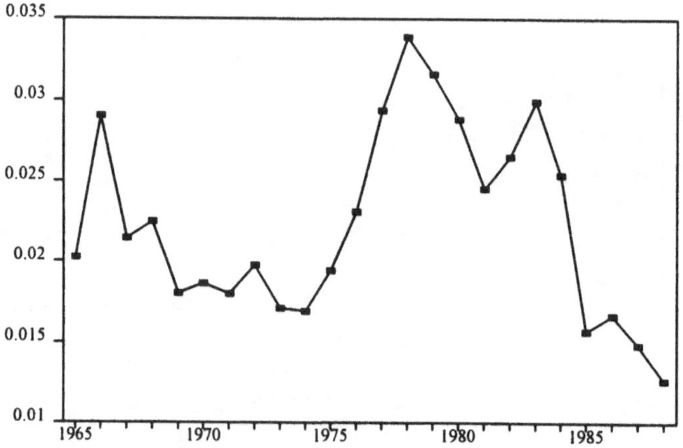

Figure 2.4 Mean TRAD7 Index: 1964-1988

Table 2.1 TRAD7 Values by Country and Means of TRAD7 and SPECL by Year 1963-1990

Year	Argentina TRAD7	Brazil TRAD7	Mexico TRAD7	Venezuela TRAD7	Chile TRAD7	Colombia TRAD7	Mean of TRAD7	Mean of SPECL
1963								0.4472
1964								0.4415
1965	0.0186	0.0093	0.0125	0.0267	0.0332	0.0211	0.0202	0.4294
1966	0.0189	0.0109	0.0154	0.0611	0.0474	0.0202	0.0290	0.4042
1967	0.0107	0.0118	0.0116	0.0512	0.0236	0.0197	0.0214	0.4159
1968	0.0120	0.0133	0.0139	0.0484	0.0293	0.0178	0.0225	0.4222
1969	0.0128	0.0126	0.0116	0.0314	0.0284	0.0112	0.0180	0.2995
1970	0.0179	0.0149	0.0123	0.0264	0.0230	0.0174	0.0186	0.3877
1971	0.0186	0.0144	0.0101	0.0216	0.0245	0.0186	0.0180	0.3816
1972	0.0156	0.0132	0.0082	0.0251	0.0423	0.0141	0.0197	0.3468
1973	0.0137	0.0121	0.0118	0.0177	0.0328	0.0145	0.0171	0.3365
1974	0.0156	0.0157	0.0187	0.0177	0.0165	0.0173	0.0169	0.3413
1975	0.0210	0.0202	0.0236	0.0182	0.0111	0.0223	0.0194	0.3067
1976	0.0243	0.0239	0.0275	0.0247	0.0104	0.0277	0.0231	0.3068
1977	0.0356	0.0253	0.0328	0.0321	0.0251	0.0253	0.0294	0.3194
1978	0.0363	0.0393	0.0368	0.0403	0.0301	0.0206	0.0339	0.3252
1979	0.0256	0.0163	0.0264	0.0679	0.0242	0.0293	0.0316	0.3020
1980	0.0352	0.0248	0.0375	0.0392	0.0177	0.0185	0.0288	0.3218
1981	0.0275	0.0171	0.0273	0.0377	0.0252	0.0125	0.0245	0.3594
1982	0.0227	0.0172	0.0182	0.0479	0.0357	0.0174	0.0265	0.3571
1983	0.0185	0.0144	0.0142	0.0486	0.0579	0.0260	0.0299	0.3457
1984	0.0142	0.0112	0.0173	0.0450	0.0396	0.0251	0.0254	0.3414
1985	0.0067	0.0064	0.0128	0.0245	0.0189	0.0247	0.0157	0.3079
1986	0.0150	0.0154	0.0186	0.0253	0.0146	0.0110	0.0167	0.2842
1987	0.0145	0.0125	0.0159	0.0239	0.0093	0.0131	0.0148	0.2850
1988	0.0112	0.0116	0.0124	0.0159	0.0094	0.0152	0.0126	0.2785
1989	0.0082	0.0071	0.0090	0.0058				
1990	0.0069	0.0064	0.0108	0.0995				

Source: authors' calculations

rate stability and reduces the likelihood of a sudden renewal of region wide debt crises triggered by movements in commodity markets. This source of risk reduction appears to be a long-run feature of economic development in the region and is fairly widespread across countries. Our results suggest that country risk analysis should place relatively greater weight on economic fundamentals and relatively less weight on political shifts in the region.

Obviously, there is no single 'Latin American' pattern of structural transformation, let alone a standard type for all developing countries. There is no reason in particular to believe that a transformation from primary products to manufactures is any more likely to be desirable than a transformation within the primary products group which recognizes more fully the country's comparative advantage. The growth performances of Chile and Argentina have not been noticeably inferior to that of Brazil and Mexico. Further examination of the relationship between growth and diversification is warranted.

It is tempting to speculate on the relationship between policy reform and patterns of diversification. The timing of Chilean diversification with the beginning of general liberalization in the mid-1970s has already been noted. The Mexican pattern of recent emphasis on machinery and motor vehicles reflects the success of the maquiladoras, which may have been fortuitously financed by the oil boom. Brazil's transition away from coffee and toward non-electrical machinery, iron and steel and transport equipment is suggestive of the relatively more import-substituting strategies followed by that country. Whether such manufacturing exports are the fruits of technological experience gained under import substitution or are mere by-products of inefficient policy-induced resource allocation remains to be seen. Is the success of Colombia in the highly competitive textile-apparel complex related to its success in managing the real exchange rate? Has the luxury of Venezuelan oil revenues combined with relative policy *dirigisme* stifled the potential for structural transformation? These are questions we hope to examine in future research.

Table 2.2 Temporal Sequencing of Exports

SITC Code		Traditionality Index	Cumulative Real Exports
Argentina			
01	Meat and preparations	0.55133	25,182
00	Live animals	0.4799	25,612
04	Cereals and preparations	0.45925	40,925
05	Fruit and vegetables	0.40884	11,389
71	Non-electrical machinery	0.3876	7,782
08	Animal feeding stuff	0.34813	16,549
42	Fixed vegetable oil, fat	0.31771	15,666
67	Iron and steel	0.30275	7,779
33	Petroleum and preparations	0.24422	10,311
22	Oil seeds, nuts, and kernels	0.23187	12,275
Brazil			
07	Coffee, tea, cocoa, spices	0.4928	93,297
00	Live animals	0.46877	42,575
06	Sugar and preparations-honey	0.46833	31,936
28	Metalliferous ores, scrap	0.34058	39,215
08	Animal feeding stuff	0.33698	31,936
33	Petroleum and products	0.30701	19,235
05	Fruit and vegetables	0.30201	20,783
71	Non-electrical machinery	0.29432	35,386
73	Transport equipment	0.2662	33,674
67	Iron and steel	0.22731	40,392
Chile			
68	Non-ferrous metals	0.49435	48,403
69	Metal manufactures nes	0.39798	2,449
67	Iron and steel	0.36496	2,387
28	Metalliferous ores, scrap	0.33895	13,995
51	Chemical elements, compounds	0.33238	2,071
25	Pulp and waste paper	0.33063	2,937
24	Wood, lumber and cork	0.30567	1,909
08	Animal feeding stuff	0.28996	5,028
05	Fruit and vegetables	0.2621	7,721
03	Fish and preparations	0.20827	2,118

Table 2.2 Continued

Colombia			
26	Textile fibers	0.48635	1,621
07	Coffee, tea, cocoa, spices	0.43855	45,140
33	Petroleum and products	0.4317	23,837
06	Sugar and preparations-honey	0.42113	1,667
66	Nonmetal mineral manufactures	0.40118	2,389
65	Textile yarn, fabric, etc.	0.38491	2,261
05	Fruit and vegetables	0.32225	4,174
29	Crude animal, vegetable materials	0.2089	2,726
84	Clothing	0.20715	2,498
32	Coal, coke, briquettes	0.13187	2,786
Mexico			
00	Live animals	0.44762	14,199
68	Non-ferrous metals	0.44624	18,951
07	Coffee, tea, cocoa, spices	0.39492	13,887
05	Fruit and vegetables	0.34671	21,272
51	Chemical elements, compounds	0.29741	11,432
67	Iron and steel	0.27074	7,431
33	Petroleum and products	0.26368	181,995
71	Non-electrical machinery	0.2078	24,774
72	electrical machinery	0.17134	24,848
73	Transport equipment	0.16782	28,760
Venezuela			
34	Natural gas and manufactures	0.62606	7,631
33	Petroleum and products	0.58466	639,321
28	Metalliferous ores, scraps	0.55055	6,626
07	Coffee, tea, cocoa, spices	0.53667	1,832
66	Nonmetal mineral manufactures	0.3358	1,352
67	Iron and steel	0.29209	5,701
51	Chemical elements, compounds	0.24778	1,880
68	Non-ferrous metals	0.23138	8,659
73	Transport equipment	0.22036	986
69	Metal manufactures, nes	0.20193	908

Real cumulative exports are in 1991 U.S. million dollars. For definition of traditionality index, see text.

References

Alam, Asad and Sarath Rajapatirana (1993), 'Trade Reform in Latin America and the Caribbean', *Finance and Development*, vol. 30, no.3.

Amin, Samir (1977), *Imperialism and Unequal Development*, Hassocks: Harvester Press.

Amin Gutiérrez de Piñeres, Sheila, and Michael J. Ferrantino (1997),'Export Diversification and Structural Dynamics in the Growth Process: The Case of Chile', *Journal of Development Economics*, Vol. 52 No. 2, April, 375-391.

Grilli, E. and C. Yang (1988), 'Primary Commodity Prices, Manufactured Goods Prices, and Terms of Trade of Developing Countries: What the Long Run Shows', *World Bank Economic Review*, vol. 2, no. 1.

Helleiner, Gerald (1986), 'Outward Orientation, Import Instability and African Economic Growth: An Empirical Investigation', in Sanjaya Lall and Frances Stewart, Eds., *Theory and Reality in Economic Development*, London: Macmillan.

Lord, Montague and Greta Boye (1991), 'The Determinants of International Trade in Latin America's Commodity Exports', in Miguel Urrutia, ed., *Long-Term Trends in Latin American Economic Development*, Baltimore: John Hopkins University Press for the Inter-American Development Bank.

Maddison, Angus (1991), 'Economic and Social Conditions in Latin America, 1913-1950', in Miguel Urrutia, ed., *Long-Term Trends in Latin American Economic Development*, Baltimore: John Hopkins University Press for the Inter-American Development Bank.

Michaely, Michael (1994), 'Trade-Preferential Agreements in Latin America: An Ex-Ante Assessment', Latin America and the Caribbean Region, World Bank, Washington, D.C.

Prebisch, Raul (1950), *The Economic Development of Latin American and Its Principal Problems*, New York: United Nations.

Prebisch, Raul (1959), 'International Trade and Payments in an Era of Coexistence Commercial Policy in the Underdeveloped Countries', *American Economic Review*, vol. 49, no. 2, pp.251-273.

Rivera, Sandra (1995), 'After NAFTA: Western Hemisphere Trade Liberalization and Alternative Paths to Integration', *Social Science Journal*, vol 32, no.4.

Sachs, Jeffery D. and Andrew Warner (1995), 'Economic Reform and the Process of Global Integration', *Brookings Papers on Economic Activity*, vol. 1, pp. 1-95.

Urrutia, Miguel (1991), 'Conclusions' in Miguel Urrutia, ed., *Long-Term Trends in Latin American Economic Development*, Baltimore: John Hopkins University Press for the Inter-American Development Bank.

3 The Commodity Composition of Export Portfolios*

Introduction

Latin American trade has boomed substantially in recent years, particularly intra-Latin trade. According to WTO data, Latin American exports to other Latin American countries, in nominal dollars, grew by 13 percent in 1991, 23 percent in 1992, 15 percent in 1993, and 14 percent in 1994, amounting to a compounded growth rate of over 16 percent over the period 1990-94. This compares with an annual growth rate of 5 percent in world exports and 6 percent in Latin American exports to the world as a whole. This rapid growth has fueled optimism about the prospects for success of the plethora of new trade liberalization initiatives in the region, including MERCOSUR and a variety of bilateral agreements.

This chapter focuses on the possible role of the commodity composition of Latin American trade in the recent Latin American export boom. Historically, these countries have specialized in primary product exports, and while substantial diversification has taken place (Amin and Ferrantino, 1997) a good deal of primary product specialization remains. The question of Latin American comparative advantage in the growth of intra-Latin trade has been particularly controversial in the context of regional integration. Yeats (1997) observed that prior to the formation of the MERCOSUR customs union among Argentina, Brazil, Paraguay and Uruguay in 1995, much of the growth of intra-MERCOSUR trade consisted of capital-intensive manufactures for which the MERCOSUR countries did not appear to have a global comparative advantage. The inference that the formation of MERCOSUR was likely to cause trade diversion has been contested (e.g. Devlin, 1996).

---

* This chapter is reprinted with some revisions by the authors from Amin Gutiérrez de Piñeres, Sheila and Michael J. Ferrantino, 'Commodity Composition of Trade: A Comparative Analysis of Latin America', *Latin American Business Review (forthcoming)*.

In order to analyze secular shifts in comparative advantage, we analyze aggregate Latin American exports to the world, constructing export similarity indices (ESIs) for seventeen Latin American and Caribbean countries (Kellner and Schroeder, 1983; Noland, 1997). Export shares of particular commodities contain most of the information in traditional indices of revealed comparative advantage based on the ratio of exports to imports, since most of the variation in these indices in practice is generated in the numerator. That is, countries buy relatively similar things from abroad, and revealed comparative advantage is driven by what countries sell abroad.

In principle, countries with dissimilar export portfolios can engage in profitable bilateral trade based on differing factor abundances and comparative costs, such as is captured by the Heckscher/Ohlin model. Countries with similar export portfolios are less likely to have such opportunities. While countries with similar portfolios of manufactured exports may enjoy efficient bilateral trade of the Helpman/Krugman type, based on product differentiation and scale economies, such opportunities seem to be limited for primary products such as bananas, coffee, and oil. The ESI thus provides circumstantial evidence to test the hypothesis that one or the other of the standard theoretical models of trade deserves relatively more weight in explaining actual trading patterns. An increasing degree of export similarity suggests that the scope for intra industry trade based on product differentiation has increased relative to that of interindustry trade based on relative factor abundance. This is particularly true if the export share of principal primary commodities has declined over time. Conversely, a declining degree of export similarity suggests that the incentives for interindustry specialization have increased relative to the incentives for intra-industry trade. While the ESI does not distinguish between various hypotheses as to *why* incentives have shifted (e.g. changes in underlying production capabilities vs. trade diversion caused by selective liberalization), it is useful in identifying the aggregate impact of all shifts in incentives to export from particular sectors among the countries involved.

Our principal findings are as follows. First, we find that broad patterns of comparative advantage remain stable over time, reflecting the continuing importance of key primary products. The grouping of Latin American countries into clusters in any year from 1962 to 1991 yields fairly similar clusters, so that the identification of particular countries with temperate agriculture, tropical agriculture, mining, or oil is fairly constant.[1] Second, within each cluster the importance of the principal primary product has decreased over time, leading to a decline in within-cluster ESI. Third, there is an increase in ESI between clusters over time, reflecting the emergence of various differentiated manufactures common to many countries' export portfolios. Fourth, there has been an increase in ESI among the three largest Latin American economies (Argentina, Brazil, and Mexico) which one would expect *a priori* to be most likely to support trade based on differentiated manufactures. These results, taken together, suggest that the incentives for intra-industry trade in manufactures among Latin American countries, based on differentiated products, have increased relative to the incentives for trade based on differing factor endowments. The emergence of intra-industry trade thus may contribute to the explanation for the acceleration of intra-Latin American trade in the 1990s.

Calculating the ESI

In constructing the ESI, we utilized two-digit SITC export data from the United Nations trade database for the years 1962-1993. The seventeen Latin American countries analyzed are Argentina, Bolivia, Brazil, Chile, Colombia, Costa Rica, Ecuador, El Salvador, Guatemala, Honduras, Jamaica, Mexico, Nicaragua, Panama, Peru, Trinidad and Tobago, and Venezuela, which among them account for the bulk of economic activity in Latin America.

The procedure for constructing the ESIs was as follows. First, we calculated the share of each two-digit SITC category in total exports for each year, using nominal dollar values. Then a series of ESI's for all seventeen country pairs for each year in the sample was constructed. The formula for the ESI between two countries, A and B, is as follows:

$$ESI(a,b) = \Sigma_i \min(X_{ia}, X_{ib})$$

where X_{ia} (X_{ib}) is industry I's export share in country a's (b's) exports.[2] The ESI varies between 0 and 1 with 1 indicating that two countries share an identical export commodity portfolio and 0 indicating a completely dissimilar portfolio. Since we analyze the export behavior of 17 countries, there are 136 distinct country pairs for which the ESI can be calculated. By constructing an annual time series of ESI, we are able to track secular changes in the index. We calculated the index from 1962 to 1993. Given reporting lags at the time we collected the data, the full 136 country pairs can be analyzed for most years including 1991, while 116 observations are available for 1992 and 55 for 1993.

Table 3.1 Countries with Most and Least Similar Exports- Top Five

LEAST SIMILAR EXPORT PORTFOLIOS[1]

1962		1982		1991	
0.004	Ecuador Venezuela	0.008	Panama Venezuela	0.041	Honduras T&T
0.004	Costa Rica Venezuela	0.012	Honduras Venezuela	0.043	Honduras Venezuela
0:005	Jamaica Venezuela	0.025	Guatemala Venezuela	0.055	Panama Venezuela
0.005	Honduras Venezuela	0.032	Nicaragua Venezuela	0.058	El Salvador Venezuela
0.006	Guatemala Venezuela	0.032	Costa Rica Venezuela	0.066	Costa Rica Venezuela

MOST SIMILAR EXPORT PORTFOLIOS

1962		1982		1991	
0.781	Panama T&T	0.715	Ecuador Mexico	0.632	Guatemala Honduras
0.813	Brazil El Salvador	0.716	Costa Rica Honduras	0.635	Guatemala Nicaragua
0.837	El Salvador Guatemala	0.750	Mexico Venezuela	0.696	El Salvador Guatemala
0.845	Brazil Guatemala	0.789	Mexico T&T	0.723	Costa Rica Honduras
0.963	T&T Venezuela	0.880	T&T Venezuela	0.784	T&T Venezuela

The abbreviation T&T indicates Trinidad and Tobago

There are also a few scattered observations missing for the 1960s. Thus, we present the evolution of intra cluster export behavior from 1962-1991, while making limited use of 1992 and 1993 data for portraying long-term trends, as shown below.

As an illustration of the behavior of the ESI across countries and over time, Table 3.1 presents the five country pairs with the most and least similar export commodity portfolios at three points in time: 1962, 1982, and 1991. The year 1982 is chosen rather than the temporal midpoint in 1977 because it represents an approximate midpoint of long-run trends in ESI for many country pairs, as will be shown below. As is readily apparent, the lowest values of the ESI occur when an oil-exporting country (Venezuela, or Trinidad and Tobago) is paired with an oil-poor country (usually a Central American country). The highest values of the ESI are consistently between the two main oil exporters, followed by pairs of countries involved in tropical agriculture (e.g. coffee).

The rankings of country pairs by ESI exhibit a fair amount of persistence over time. The Pearson correlation coefficient between ESIs in 1962 and 1991 is fairly high at .5736. Nine of the 25 most similar pairs are the same for both 1962 and 1991 (one would expect 4.6 by random chance). For 121 of the 136 country pairs, the annual variance of the ESI over the 30 years is less than .02. In fifteen other cases, the annual variance of the ESI ranges from .02 to nearly .07. Seven of these cases involve Ecuador, for which the importance of oil has risen and declined substantially over the period.

Identifying the Commodity Clusters

For each year, we performed a cluster analysis on the vector of export shares X_i. which underly the calculations of ESI. The purpose of this analysis was to identify groups of countries which export relatively similar products. We used a variety of clustering algorithms (Ward's minimum distance, average linkage, centroid, McQuitty's similarity analysis, Gower's median method). Although there is some variation among the results of the different methods, fifteen of the seventeen the countries consistently fit into four clusters in most years and using most methods. The four primary clusters are as follows:

- A *tropical agriculture* cluster, whose predominant exports include coffee, fruit and vegetables, and consisting of Brazil, Colombia, Costa Rica, Ecuador, El Salvador, Guatemala, and Honduras;

- A *temperate agriculture* cluster, with relative specialization in textile fibers, cereals, and meat, including Argentina, Mexico, and Nicaragua;
- *mining* cluster, specialized in metalliferous ores, nonferrous metals and (secondarily) in animal feeding stuff, consisting of Bolivia, Chile, and Peru;
- An *oil* cluster, made up of Trinidad and Tobago and Venezuela.

Jamaica and Panama stand alone as *sui generis* single-country clusters, with Jamaica concentrated in chemical elements and metalliferous ores, while Panama shifts from being an oil exporter early in the period to a specialization in fruits, vegetables, and fish later in the period. Cluster membership tends to be relatively stable over time regardless of the algorithm chosen, with the greatest shifts in membership involving countries for which exports of oil have either risen or declined in importance over the period (Ecuador, Mexico, and Panama).

Tables 3.2 through 3.6 show the principal 2-digit SITC categories of each cluster's exports during 1962, 1982, and 1991, selected according to the unweighted mean across the cluster, as well as the shares for each member of the cluster. For each cluster, it can be seen that the 1962 pattern of specialization persists at least partially in 1991, particularly for the oil exporting countries. Also, in each cluster, the weight of the most important primary export commodities has decreased over time.

For example, consider the tropical agriculture cluster (Table 3.2). The share of coffee, tea, etc. (SITC 28: hereinafter 'coffee') dropped from 50.5 percent to 20 percent for the average country in the group, with the move out of coffee being the main engine of diversification. Honduras is the only country to show an increase in the share of coffee exports in total exports. Fruits/vegetables still remains second to coffee in primary importance with its share fairly consistent at about 18 percent. The tropical agriculture cluster also shows a relative increase in the importance of labor-intensive and intermediate-goods manufacturing exports (such as clothing, dyes, and iron/steel) and a relative decline in the exports of primary inputs into intermediate-goods manufacturing (such as textile fibers, wood, and metallic ores). These primary goods are likely being increasingly absorbed domestically in production of the corresponding manufactured goods, rather than being exported. Meat and sugar are also significant for the group as a whole, reflecting their importance in the Central American countries.

Table 3.2 Tropical Agriculture Cluster*

Year	SITC	Industry	BR	CO	CR	EC	ES	GU	HO	Mean
1962	07	coffee	0.576	0.725	0.580	0.341	0.562	0.604	0.150	0.505
1962	05	f/v	0.017	0.023	0.231	0.580	0.003	0.073	0.494	0.203
1962	26	tex. fibers	0.117	0.035	0.001	0.000	0.239	0.136	0.028	0.079
1962	24	wood	0.034	0.005	0.003	0.011	0.000	0.010	0.094	0.022
1962	28	met. ores	0.083	0.000	0.000	0.000	0.000	0.000	0.065	0.021
1982	07	coffee	0.132	0.523	0.296	0.123	0.299	0.344	0.239	0.279
1982	05	f/v	0.037	0.056	0.305	0.098	0.016	0.115	0.378	0.144
1982	33	oil	0.071	0.071	0.007	0.653	0.032	0.000	0.001	0.119
1982	26	tex. fibers	0.008	0.009	0.000	0.004	0.117	0.080	0.010	0.032
1982	65	textiles	0.026	0.029	0.022	0.001	0.100	0.039	0.010	0.032
1991	07	coffee	0.060	0.195	0.168	0.079	0.366	0.266	0.269	0.200
1991	05	f/v	0.038	0.070	0.326	0.258	0.011	0.115	0.412	0.176
1991	33	oil	0.013	0.201	0.005	0.406	0.000	0.019	0.000	0.092
1991	03	meat	0.005	0.024	0.038	0.202	0.040	0.016	0.081	0.058
1991	06	sugar	0.015	0.012	0.015	0.004	0.071	0.134	0.000	0.036

* We are employing the following abbreviations: BR- Brazil; CO- Colombia; CR- Costa Rica; EC- Ecuador; ES- El Salvador; GU-Guatemala; HO-Honduras; met. ores -metalliferous ores, tex.fibers- textile fibers, and f/v - fruits/vegetables.

Table 3.3 Temperate Agriculture Cluster

Year	SITC	Industry	Argentina	Mexico	Nicaragua	Mean
1962	26	textile fibers	0.147	0.226	0.380	0.251
1962	07	coffee	0.003	0.092	0.234	0.110
1962	04	cereals	0.290	0.012	0.013	0.105
1962	01	meat	0.188	0.030	0.074	0.097
1962	68	nonferrous metals	0.003	0.108	0.048	0.053
1982	33	oil	0.071	0.748	0.017	0.279
1982	07	coffee	0.005	0.019	0.434	0.152
1982	26	textile fibers	0.039	0.010	0.300	0.116
1982	04	cereals	0.241	0.000	0.000	0.080
1982	03	fish	0.025	0.019	0.075	0.040
1991	33	oil	0.060	0.288	0.013	0.120
1991	01	meat	0.074	0.001	0.158	0.078
1991	05	fruits/vegetables	0.057	0.056	0.116	0.076
1991	26	textile fibers	0.029	0.008	0.184	0.074
1991	73	transport equipment	0.022	0.170	0.000	0.064

Table 3.4 Mining Cluster

Year	SITC	Industry	Bolivia	Chile	Peru	Mean
1962	28	metalliferous ores	0.913	0.156	0.159	0.410
1962	68	nonferrous metals	0.000	0.666	0.261	0.309
1962	26	textile fibers	0.000	0.011	0.218	0.076
1962	08	animal feeding stuff	0.000	0.016	0.210	0.075
1962	07	coffee	0.048	0.000	0.050	0.033
1982	68	nonferrous metals	0.518	0.379	0.264	0.387
1982	28	metalliferous ores	0.363	0.238	0.153	0.251
1982	33	oil	0.000	0.020	0.269	0.096
1982	08	animal feeding stuff	0.000	0.076	0.031	0.036
1982	05	fruits/vegetables	0.006	0.076	0.008	0.030
1991	68	nonferrous metals	0.189	0.347	0.290	0.276
1991	28	metalliferous ores	0.404	0.139	0.166	0.236
1991	08	animal feeding stuff	0.042	0.057	0.150	0.083
1991	05	fruits/vegetables	0.033	0.115	0.029	0.059
1991	24	wood	0.072	0.031	0.001	0.035

Table 3.5 Oil Cluster

Year	SITC	Industry	Trinidad & Tobago	Venezuela	Mean
1962	33	oil	0.862	0.925	0.893
1962	06	sugar	0.062	0.000	0.031
1962	67	iron/steel	0.000	0.048	0.024
1962	07	coffee	0.016	0.011	0.014
1962	56	fertilizers-manufactured	0.014	0.000	0.007
1982	33	oil	0.874	0.956	0.915
1982	51	chemical elements	0.042	0.006	0.024
1982	68	non ferrous metals	0.000	0.018	0.009
1982	73	transport equipment	0.017	0.001	0.009
1982	67	iron/steel	0.010	0.005	0.007
1991	33	oil	0.612	0.803	0.707
1991	51	chemical elements	0.166	0.013	0.089
1991	67	iron/steel	0.062	0.031	0.047
1991	68	non ferrous metals	0.000	0.049	0.024
1991	56	fertilizers-manufactured	0.032	0.004	0.018

Table 3.6 Outliers: Jamaica and Panama

Year	SITC	Industry	Jamaica	Panama	Mean
1962	05	fruits/vegetables	0.109	0.409	0.259
1962	28	metalliferous ores	0.493	0.009	0.251
1962	33	oil	0.000	0.481	0.240
1962	06	sugar	0.252	0.000	0.126
1962	07	coffee	0.035	0.066	0.051
1982	51	chemical elements	0.491	0.000	0.245
1982	05	fruits/ vegetables	0.035	0.310	0.172
1982	03	fish	0.000	0.264	0.132
1982	28	metalliferous ores	0.182	0.000	0.091
1982	06	sugar	0.067	0.108	0.088
1991	51	chemical elements	0.524	0.011	0.267
1991	05	fruits/ vegetables	0.063	0.338	0.200
1991	03	fish	0.003	0.230	0.116
1991	84	clothing	0.082	0.072	0.077
1991	28	metalliferous ores	0.109	0.008	0.059

The temperate agriculture cluster (Table 3.3) includes the two large economies of Argentina and Mexico, as well as Nicaragua. These countries as a group initially exhibited more diversification than the tropical-agriculture countries. In 1962, the cluster-average share of the top three export categories in total exports was only 36.6 percent percent in the temperate agriculture cluster compared with 78.7 percent in the tropical- agriculture cluster. Diversification continued throughout the period under analysis. The cluster-average shares of the principal 1962 exports, textile fibers and coffee/tea, fell from 25.1 percent and 11.0 percent respectively to 1991 levels of 7.4 percent and 6 percent in 1991. Cereals, which was the third most important export in 1962, is not in the top ten by 1991. Argentina and Mexico show movement out of primary products into higher-end manufactures, such as transport equipment and nonelectrical machinery. Oil continues as Mexico's largest export but has been volatile; its share rose from 3 percent of Mexico's exports in 1972 to 75 percent in 1982, then retreated sharply to 29 percent by 1991. Nicaragua's exports are still concentrated in meat, textile fibers, coffee, and sugar, but show signs of diversifying.

In the mining cluster (Table 3.4), ores and nonferrous metals still are the largest exports, but with a relatively rapid diversification into manufactured exports. A similar, but more modest, expansion of manufactured exports is observable in the temperate agriculture cluster. In Bolivia, ores and metals accounted for 91.3 percent of exports in 1962, declining to 60.3 percent in 1991. In the case of Peru exports are still concentrated in ores, metals and animal feeding stuff, with the textiles-clothing complex comprising 10 percent of Peruvian exports in 1991. Among the mining countries, Chile shows the strongest trend towards diversification. Metals and ores were 82.2 percent of exports in 1962, but by 1991 had fallen to 48.6 percent of the total. Since its extensive program of liberalization in the 1970s, Chile's exports of 'non-traditional' primary products such as fruits/vegetables, wood, and fish, have increased in importance.

The move towards diversification has been weakest in the oil cluster (Table 3.5). The share of oil in total exports from 1962-1991 declined only from 92.5 percent to 80.3 percent in Venezuela, and from 86.2 percent to 61.2 percent in Trinidad and Tobago. Apparently, the revenue generated by oil exports suppresses countries' ability to diversify and expand their comparative advantage. The peculiarity of oil may be that its production is relatively intensive in capital and skilled labor compared to coffee or fruit. This may make the 'Dutch disease' phenomenon of resources being drawn out of other sectors into the primary export commodity more costly for oil exporters than for agricultural exporters. In light of the experience in Venezuela and Trinidad, the Mexican experience of successful expansion of diversified manufacturing exports (associated in large measure with the maquiladora program), while simultaneously operating a large export oil sector, is all the more noteworthy. Jamaica and Panama (Table 3.6) are both outliers, whose patterns of comparative advantage are not easily classified. In Jamaica, the dominance of 'metalliferous ores', giving way to 'chemical elements', reflects the development of downstream stages of the processing of bauxite into aluminum. In Panama, significant oil exports in the early decades have dried up; except for these, the cluster analysis would have probably placed Panama with the other Central American countries on the strength of its exports of fruits/vegetables and fish.

In summary, most Latin American countries have shown increasing export diversification in recent decades, with diversification encompassing a larger range of primary products in some cases and proceeding from primary products to manufactures in other cases. The pace of diversification has been most rapid for countries specializing in mining and tropical agriculture, moderate for countries specializing in temperate agriculture, and relatively slow for oil exporters.

Trends in Export Similarity By Cluster

Figure 3.1 shows the secular trend of unweighted average export similarity among the 136 country pairs in the analysis.[3] The mean value of the export similarity index has increased from about .233 to .287 in the last 30 years, suggesting convergence in patterns of comparative advantage. This movement represents a fairly steady secular trend, with the exception of the period from 1975 to 1982. The ESI rose sharply from .263 in 1975 to .343 in 1978, dropping back to .264 in 1982. This boom-and-bust behavior of export similarity could be due either to an over extension and retrenchment of manufactures, or to sharply rising and falling prices for principal primary products.

Of the 136 country pairs, 28 involve pairs of countries sharing a cluster while 108 are pairs of countries between clusters. Figure 3.2 decomposes the trend of export similarity into its within-cluster and between-cluster components. Within-cluster similarity has declined steadily, from levels exceeding .5 in the 1960s to about .39 in the 1990s. Unsurprisingly, as it accounts for the bulk of observations, between-cluster similarity follows more or less the pattern of aggregate similarity, rising from .167 in 1962 to .259 in 1991, and showing a pattern of accelerating and decelerating relative to trend in the late 1970s and early 1980s. More interesting is the convergence between within-cluster and between-cluster means; the difference between the two which declines from .322 in 1962 to .134 in 1993. The distinctions between countries in terms of specialization are substantially less than previously.

Thus, convergence among the export patterns of Latin American countries has taken place simultaneously with a decline in the importance of most countries' single principal primary commodity. The convergence thus must be attributed at least in part to increasing exports of manufactures, and perhaps in part also to an increase in non-traditional forms of agriculture which are less location-specific than tropical crops such as coffee and sugar.

Figure 3.3 illustrates a similar pattern of trend convergence among the three largest Latin American economies (Argentina, Brazil, and Mexico). Though the series is more volatile due to the small number of observations (three), the overshooting and reversion to trend in the late 1970s and early 1980s also occurs for this subset of countries. The reoccurrence of the aggregate pattern for the large, diversified economies makes it more likely that the behavior of manufactures is important in explaining both the long-term trend and the mid-series anomaly.

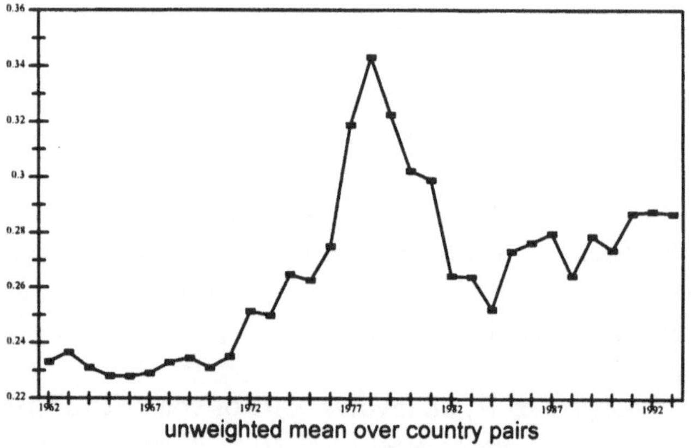

Figure 3.1 Export Similarity in Latin America

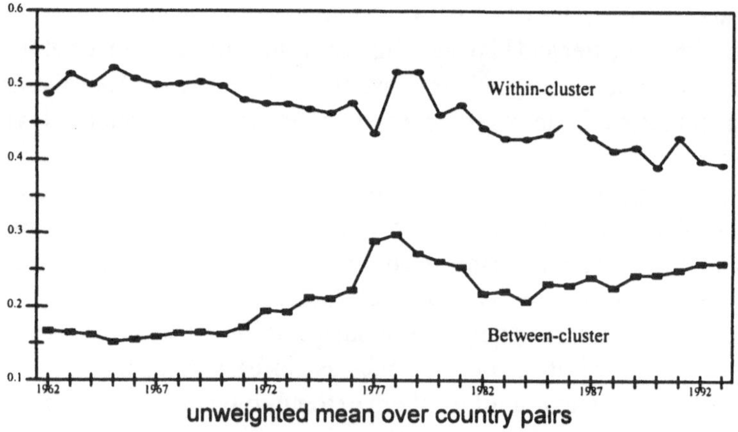

Figure 3.2 Similarity Within and Between Clusters

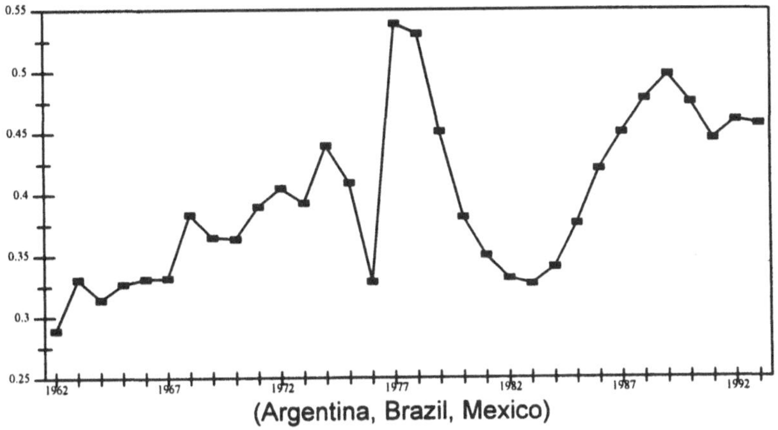

Figure 3.3 'Big 3' Export Similarity

Conclusion

We have found a secular pattern of convergence among the export patterns of Latin American countries, and a simultaneous decline in the importance of traditional primary products. These patterns, together with the recent rapid growth in intra-Latin trade, are difficult to reconcile with the idea that such trade is based primarily on Heckscher/Ohlin type specialization based on different factor endowments. There is at least some circumstantial evidence that Helpman/Krugman type of bilateral trade in similar manufacturing categories, based on product differentiation and scale economies, such as characterizes trade among the developed countries, may account for part of the recent acceleration in intra-Latin trade. As noted earlier, on the basis of the present data alone it is difficult to distinguish between the hypothesis of increasing efficient trade based on product differentiation and scale economies and the alternate hypothesis that selective trade liberalization may have induced trade diversion in favor of intra-Latin trade in manufactures.

Based on the export similarity index, the strongest opportunities for Heckscher/Ohlin trade of dissimilar products, based on comparative costs, appear to be between the oil exporters, on the one hand, and the rest of Latin America, on the other. It remains fairly difficult to exchange coffee for coffee, or bananas for bananas. The Central American countries continue to resemble one another strongly in their pattern of comparative advantage, with the apparent natural scope for trade among them being relatively limited, and relatively little structural change has taken place in the oil exporters. Brazil, Colombia, Chile, and Mexico have all experienced substantial structural transformation as described above.

From a policy standpoint, it is useful to note that the recent diversification has taken place in all types of Latin American economies, and has proceeded fairly steadily over time. With the possible exception of oil, the export sectors of Latin American economies continue to diversify regardless of their original resource endowments, and regardless of whether import-substitution or neoclassical policies have been followed. It may be that this is a general rule of development which would apply to developing countries outside of Latin America. If so, then the potential gains (if any) from policies deliberately aimed at bringing about diversification may be limited, as such policies would only accelerate trends which are taking place anyway, and would likely be less efficient in selecting new export sectors than an undirected market mechanism. Also, the uniformity of the observed pattern of diversification and convergence, encompassing countries which have pursued varying strategies of trade liberalization, makes it at least somewhat less likely that trade diversion in the MERCOSUR customs union is a unicausal explanation for the patterns we observe. In turn, this implies that caution is in order in inferring that MERCOSUR has induced costly trade diversion based on recent shifts in trade patterns alone.

The question of whether the recent boom in intra-Latin trade reflects structural transformation in the region's economies, trade diversion, or both, remains an open one. Further progress awaits the assembling of usable time-series data on tariffs and non-tariff barriers for these countries. Such data is relatively scarce even for developed countries, and even more so for developing countries, though the Inter-American Development Bank has recently made some progress in this area. Given the rapid liberalizations taking place in Latin America in recent years, and the confusing proliferation of bilateral and plurilateral free-trade agreements with different time tables and product coverage, it will no doubt be some time before the effects of Latin American trade policy in the current episode can be empirically unscrambled from other changes occurring simultaneously in these economies.

Notes

1. This is consistent with the finding of Gagnon and Rose (1995) that patterns of comparative advantage for both developed and non-Latin-American developing countries are persistent over long periods of time.
2. Earlier applications of this measure include Finger and Kreinen (1979), Kellman and Schroeder (1983), Pearson (1994), and Nolan (1997).
3. In order to extend the graph to 1993, missing values for 1992 and 1993 were set equal to the most recent lagged value. This was considered reasonable due to the relative stability of the series. If the first difference of the data are randomly distributed across pairs, the estimates of the averages should be unbiased but may display less volatility than would averages using full-sample data.

References

Amin Gutiérrez de Piñeres, Sheila and Michael J. Ferrantino (1997) 'Export Diversification and Structural Change: Some Comparisons for Latin America', *The International Executive*, July/August 1997.

Devlin, Robert (1996), 'In Defense of Mercosur', *The IDB* (December 3), Washington, DC: Inter-American Development Bank.

Finger, J. Michael and Mordecai E. Kreinin (1979), 'A Measure of "Export Similarity" and Its Possible Uses', *Economic Journal*, vol. 89, pp. 905-12.

Gagnon, Joseph E. and Andrew K. Rose (1995), 'Dynamic Persistence of Industry Trade Balances: How Pervasive is the Product Cycle?', *Oxford Economic Papers*, vol. 47:2 pp. 29-248.

Kellman, Mitchell and Tim Schroeder (1983), 'The Export Similarity Index: Some Structural Tests', *Economic Journal*, vol. 93, pp. 193-8.

Noland, Marcus (1997), 'Has Asian Export Performance Been Unique?', *Journal of International Economics*, vol. 43, no. ½ (August), pp.79-102.

Pearson, Charles (1994), 'The Asian Export Ladder', in Shu-Chin Yang ed., *Manufactured Exports of East Asian Industrializing Economics*, Amonk: M.E. Sharpe.

United Nations *International Trade Statistics Yearbook*, various years

Yeats, Alexander (1997), 'Does Mercosur's Trade Performance Raise Concerns About the Effects of Regional Trade Arrangements?', *World Bank Policy Research Working Paper*, No. 1729 (February), Washington, DC: World Bank.

4 Export Diversification and Structural Dynamics in the Growth Process: The case of Chile*

Introduction

The literature on export-led growth in developing countries has burgeoned in recent years. Alongside the hypothesis that outward-oriented countries grow more rapidly is another hypothesis, that the pattern of economic development is associated with structural change in exports and increased export diversification. The hypothesis of diversification-led development is not necessarily tied to the outward-orientation hypothesis. For example, in the well-known model of development through industrialization (Rosenstein-Rodan 1943; Prebisch 1950; Singer 1950, 1952; Nurske 1953) infant industries encouraged by protection and import substitution also would increase diversification in the economy. The 'non-traditional' industries are presumed to be manufacturing industries, and since the protection is presumed to be temporary, diversification in production eventually leads to diversification in exports and an escape from the 'primary-product' trap.

Other models of trade and growth, in very different traditions, also imply a link between export diversification and the development process. For example, in the product-cycle literature (Vernon 1966; Krugman 1979; Dollar 1986; Segerstrom, Anant and Dinopolous 1990; Grossman and Helpman 1991, ch. 12), innovative activity by the North leads to an increasing diversity of products, while imitative activity by the South leads to an increasing diversity of products being produced and exported from low-wage locations, Thus,

* This chapter printed with some revisions by the authors Amin Gutiérrez de Piñeres, Sheila and Michael J. Ferrantino, 'Export Diversification and Structural Dynamics in the Growth Process: A Case of Chile', *Journal of Development Economics,* April 1997, vol. 52, no. 2, pp. 375-391.

general growth, export growth and diversification are linked. Learning-curve processes and knowledge spillovers are believed to play an important role in this process (Amin Gutiérrez de Piñeres, 1996).

Furthermore, the large volume of trade between developed countries with similar factor endowments has been explained in terms of product differentiation, usually associated with manufacturing (Krugman 1981; Helpman and Krugman 1985). Markusen (1986) has proposed an East-West-South model of trade in which developing countries export undifferentiated goods based on factor advantages while developed countries export differentiated products. Presumably, the process of 'graduation' from LDC to DC status experienced by some countries should be accompanied by a structural change of exports in the direction of diversity. The empirical results of Michaely (1977) and Moschos (1989), among others, which find that the link between exports and growth kicks in after a certain threshold of development, are suggestive of such a graduation process.

In light of the widespread implicit prediction of a link between diversification, export growth, and aggregate development, it is surprising that little has been done to test this hypothesis directly. In this chapter we hope to contribute something towards filling this lacuna. Of course, the link between aggregate exports and aggregate growth has been examined numerous times, with mixed results. This literature has been ably reviewed by Edwards (1993). While much has been learned by these methods, the examination of aggregates limits the type of statements which can be made about diversification or structural change. Furthermore, the methodological progression from relatively simple methods (Emery 1967; Kravis 1970; Krueger 1978; Balassa 1978) through Granger-Sims type methods (Jung and Marshall 1985; Bahmani-Oskooee et al. 1991; Esfahani 1991; Serletis 1992) and on through cointegration have continued to focus on either contemporaneous or relatively short-term shocks (a few quarters, or one or two years) in the exports-output relationship. The unfolding of structural change in exports as suggested by any of the above models, or others that might be proposed, requires a longer perspective.

The present contribution examines the Chilean experience with exports and growth by constructing several measures of diversification and structural change in Chilean exports from disaggregated data over a thirty-year period. Then, using these measures we test a number of relationships among the structure of exports, export growth, Chilean growth, and world growth. By looking at the evolution and structural change of exports by sector over the long run, we find a number of interesting results. First, the degree of export diversification in Chile increased sharply from about 1975 onwards, with the process of diversification being essentially completed by 1988. Second, a crude association of 'traditionality' with primary products and 'non-traditionality' with manufactures fails to represent the Chilean experience. As Chile emerged from an import-substitution period into a period of freer trade, its true comparative advantage was more visibly expressed; thus, some manufactured exports declined while some primary products grew. Third, the short-run dynamics of diversification and structural change show a marked pattern. Most change in the composition of Chilean exports has taken place during periods of internal crisis or external shock. During stable interim periods, diversification has *not* taken place, growth has been relatively good, and the link between world growth and Chilean exports has been stronger. This suggests that if there is a long-run relationship between growth and export diversification it is of a start-and-stop nature, resembling the 'punctuated equilibria' currently in vogue in evolutionary biology.

Historical Overview of the Chilean Economy

Useful and detailed surveys of Chilean development at various phases of the process are provided by Behrman (1976), Foxley (1983), and Edwards and Edwards (1987). For the present purpose, we need to emphasize several salient facts. The first is the pattern of relatively high long-run growth punctuated by crisis. Annual growth rates of GDP averaged 4.3 percent for the years 1963-1972 (although other Latin American economies grew faster), 5.9 percent for the years 1976-1981, and 5.4 percent for the years 1984-1991. This performance was interrupted by three sharp contractions in output. The first, in 1973, was associated with the collapse of the brief experiment with socialism and nationalization under Dr. Salvador Allende, ending in the September coup. The second, in 1975, was the result of the 'shock therapy' treatment of inflation administered by the monetarist policy makers which came into power under Gen. Augusto Pinochet. The third, in 1982-1983, was associated with the general debt crisis in Latin America, as unsustainable foreign borrowing met the constraints of rising oil prices, rising real interest rates, and falling copper prices.

The long-run growth performance described above took place under the background of a wide variety of policy experiments. In the 1950s and 1960s, Chile pursued a strategy of import substitution in accordance with the Prebisch/Singer line then current in Latin America. This began with the establishment of a number of heavy industries under the CORFO (*Corporacion de Fomento de la Producción*) and continued with the establishment of a variety of tariffs giving Chile a high level of aggregate protection and an erratic pattern of effective protection, biased against agriculture (Behrman, 1976, Ch. 5). The chronic overvaluation of the exchange rate was combated by intermittent attempts at liberalization during 1956-1967, 1959-1961 and 1965-1970 (Behrman, Ch. 13).

The Unidad Popular government of Dr. Allende (November 1970-September 1973) originally maintained a high growth rate by means of rapidly rising fiscal deficits, which grew from 3 percent of GDP in 1970 to 13 percent in 1972 and 24 percent in 1973. At first it was believed that these deficits would be non-inflationary due to the presence of excess capacity. But as the money supply expanded at triple-digit rates, price controls led to the repression of inflation and widespread black markets, finally culminating in food rationing (the 'popular basket'). The nationalization of numerous firms, usually preceded by long strikes and seizure of plant and equipment by workers, led to losses in most cases. A severe depletion of foreign exchange in early 1973 led to exchange controls, fifteen separate official exchange rates, and confiscatory deposits on imports. After the opposition scored sizable gains in the March 1973 parliamentary elections, the internal conflict was suddenly terminated in the September 11 coup.

Under the military regime, Chile embarked on a number of remarkable experiments designed to bring the country in line with the principles of laissez-faire and monetarism as advocated by a group of U.S.-trained policy makers known popularly as the 'Chicago boys'. The first wave of these policies includedan initial massive devaluation, the decontrol of many domestic prices, the establishment of new private lending institutions with decontrolled interest rates (the *financerias*), the privatization of much of the CORFO portfolio, leading to the establishment of large conglomerates or *grupos*, and large layoffs of civil servants. Beginning in 1975, a policy of gradual reduction of money supply growth and sharp fiscal tightening lowered the inflation rate from 605.9 percent in 1973 to an eventual 9.9 percent in 1981. An initial total abolition of import quotas was coupled with an eventual tariff reduction causing the average nominal tariff to fall from 94 percent in 1973 to 10.1 percent in 1979, with only automobiles being exempted from the 10 percent maximum tariff.

In the late 1970s, several changes of course took place in the policy mix. Emphasis shifted from money supply control to exchange rate control. The establishment of a series of automatic exchange rate reductions (the *tablita*) was meant to bring the peso mechanically to its purchasing-power-parity level but led to progressive overvaluation. After initially following a policy of repressing union activity, the government acceded to 100 percent wage indexation for union workers, in part as a political tradeoff for sweeping deregulation of health, social security and education. This support of urban purchasing power, coupled with the liberalization of the capital account in 1979 and low tariffs, led to unsustainable foreign borrowing and the payments crisis of the early 1980s. Widespread bankruptcies ensued, with public awareness heightened by the 1981 failure of the CRAV *grupo*. In late 1982 the Pinochet government approached the IMF seeking emergency assistance, and in return imposed a typical stabilization program, including devaluation. After a disruptive episode involving nationalization and liquidation of banks as well as widespread fraud investigations regarding the heavy extension of credits by banks to *grupos*, the path toward reform once again resumed. The general trend toward liberalization continued even as protests against the military government increased, and was reaffirmed after the democratic election of Patricio Aylwin in 1989.

Data and Analysis

We analyzed two-digit export data from the United Nations trade database for the years 1962-1991 in an attempt to derive empirical measures of the 'traditionality' of specific export industries as well as measures of the degree of export diversification and structural change taking place in Chile's export portfolio. Let e_{it} represent exports by Chilean industry I in year t, expressed in constant (1982) U.S. dollars. As a first step, we calculated a cumulative export experience function for each commodity. This is obtained as:

$$c_{it} = \frac{\sum_{i,t_0}^{t} e_{it}}{\sum_{i,t_0}^{t_1} e_{it}}$$

where t_0 and t_1 represent the initial and terminal periods of the sample. In this case the calculation has been performed over the period 1962-1991.
The variable c_{it} has properties similar to that of a cumulative distribution function; it takes on values at or near 0 at the beginning of the sample period and rises to 1 in the final year. If values of c_{it} for two different industries were plotted together, an industry whose export experience was concentrated earlier in the period (a 'traditional' industry) would be differentiated from an industry whose export experience was concentrated later in the period (a 'non-traditional' industry) in that its export experience function would be shifted to the left.

Figure 4.1 illustrates cumulative distribution functions for five of the more important Chilean export industries, these being non-ferrous metals; chemical elements and compounds; wood, lumber and cork; fruit and vegetables; and fish. The most traditional of the five industries, non-ferrous metals, has a cumulative distribution function shifted to the left, indicating that a large proportion of the exports occurred relatively early in the sample period. The nearly linear shape of the function for non-ferrous metals reflects the fact that real exports are roughly constant over the sample period. The non-traditional industries of fruit and vegetables have functions shifted to the right, indicating more export experience in recent years. In general, the more rapidly real exports have grown in a given industry, the more the graph of C_{it} will be shifted to the right.

The null hypothesis that two industries have identical cumulative export experience functions can be tested against the alternative that one of the industries is more 'traditional' in several ways. The most straightforward method of ranking exports by traditionality is to construct the mean of the cumulative export experience index for each industry as:

$$T_i = \frac{\sum_{t\,t_0}^{t_1} c_{it}}{t_1 - t_0 + 1}$$

More traditional industries have a higher score for T_i. We calculated traditionality scores T_i for the full set of 54 two-digit export industries. These are presented in Table 4.1.

The rankings for the industries where we tried both methods are comparable, indicating that the historical record of structural change is easy to identify. Also, it is easy again to reject the null hypothesis that all exports followed the same pattern of historical growth. For example, 'rubber manufactures n.e.s.', the 17th least traditional industry, is less traditional than 'transport equipment', the 36th least traditional industry, at a significance level of .05, while it is possible to distinguish the 20th least traditional industry,

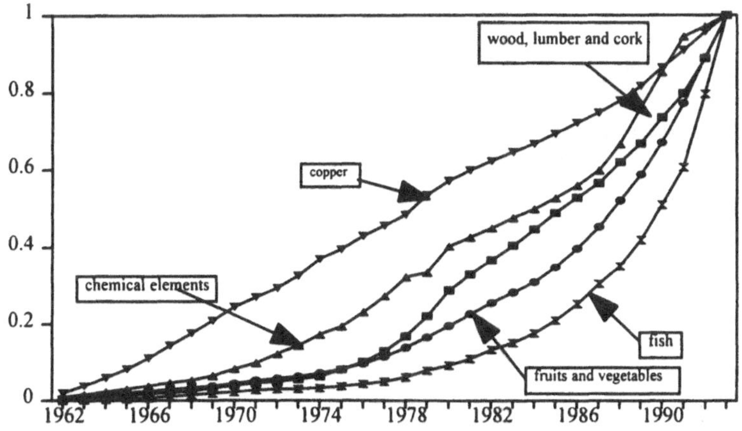

Figure 4.1 Cumulative Exports

'dyes and tanning', from the 32nd least traditional industry, 'petroleum and products', at a significance level of .1.[1]

Parts of the Chilean story, such as the shift from reliance on copper and nitrates toward flowers and fruit, can be readily identified in Table 4.1. An important general point about these patterns is that it is a mistake to identify primary products with 'traditionality' and manufacturing with 'non-traditionality', as some analysts have done, and to assume that a country exporting more manufactures is evolving in the direction of its true comparative advantage. In Chile, primary products industries including tobacco, coffee and tea, and dairy products are among the newest successful exporters, while plastics, manufactured fertilizers, electrical and non-electrical machinery and miscellaneous metal manufactures are relatively 'traditional' when the historical record is examined, and clearly possess less dynamism.[2]

We generated three measures of the composition of exports, which capture medium-run structural change, short-run structural change and static specialization/diversification, respectively. The first measure, TRAD7, is the variance of the traditionality index calculated across industries, but using seven-year intervals rather than the full sample period.[3] Thus, we have values of TRAD7 for 1965-1988; the value of 1965, e.g. is the variance of the 54 industry values of T_i obtained using the period 1962-1968 as a reference period. When the variance is high, this implies that the industries experienced relatively divergent patterns of export growth during the period, with some being leaders and some laggers, so that a high variance is interpreted as an episode of structural change centered on the period in question. A low variance implies that the composition of exports was relatively stable over the 7-year period.

The second measure, CSX, is a measure of the change in export composition taking place in a single year. It is calculated as:

$$CSX = \sum_{i=1}^{54} \min(s_{i,t}, s_{i,t-1})$$

where $s_{it} = e_{it} / \sum_{I \in (1,54)} e_{it}$, the share of industry I's exports in national exports in year t.[4] CSX takes on a maximum value of 1 if there is no change in export composition while it takes on a minimum value of 0 if a country exports a

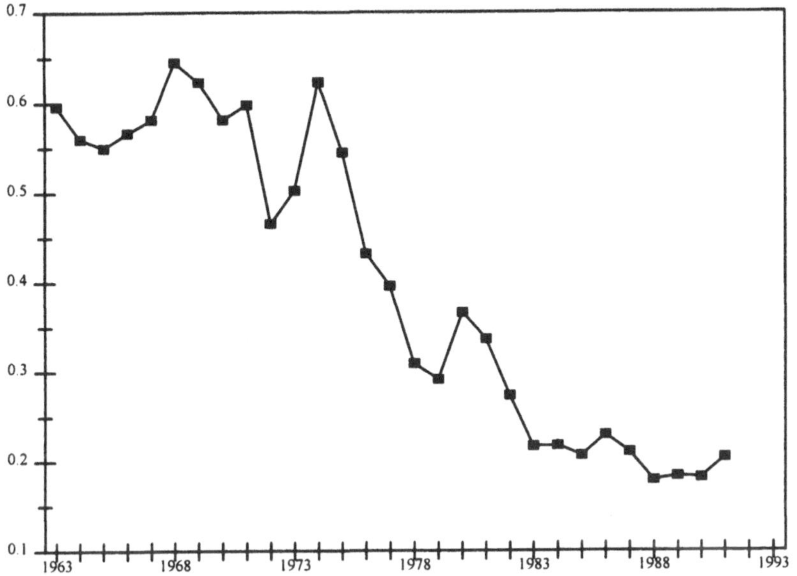

Figure 4.2 Specialization Index

portfolio of goods, none of which were exported in the previous year. High values of CSX indicate short-run stability in export composition.

Finally, a static measure of specialization, SPECL, is calculated as

$$SPECL_t = \sum_{i=1}^{54} (s_{i,t})^2$$

in a manner analogous to the Herfindahl-Hirschman index used to measure industrial concentration. A score approaching 1 implies reliance on a single export (a high degree of specialization) while a score approaching 0 implies a high degree of export diversification. Figure 4.2 shows the behavior of the

Table 4.1 Temporal Sequencing of Chilean Real Export 1962-1991

Rank	U.N. Code	Industry	Traditionality Index	Variance of Traditionality Index	Cumulative Real Exports 1991 U.S. $ (thousands)
1	12	Tobacco and manufactures	0.06863	0.04250	24471
2	7	Coffee, tea, cocoa, spices	0.07089	0.04041	67093
3	94	Zoo animals, pets	0.09833	0.04436	5456
4	42	Fixed vegetable oil, fat	0.10328	0.06420	3328
5	9	Misc. food preparations	0.10846	0.06960	44873
6	84	Clothing	0.11278	0.05406	150503
7	2	Dairy products and eggs	0.12890	0.07576	35443
8	23	Rubber, crude & synthetic	0.13104	0.10276	43111
9	63	Wood, cork manufactures, n.e.s.	0.14518	0.05916	658011
10	82	Furniture	0.15285	0.05451	74951
11	54	Medicinal products, etc.	0.15547	0.04723	36057
12	55	Perfume, cleaning products etc.	0.16433	0.07258	70013
13	85	Footwear	0.16489	0.05192	127608
14	62	Rubber manufactures, n.e.s.	0.17583	0.06138	134372
15	53	Dyes, tanning, colour products	0.20468	0.07650	16926
16	1	Meat and preparations	0.20543	0.08289	180218
17	3	Fish and preparations	0.20827	0.07112	2117869
18	83	Travel goods, handbags	0.21419	0.06013	3160
19	65	Textile yarn, fabric, etc.	0.22003	0.08167	209934
20	11	Beverages	0.22109	0.05574	571514
21	93	Special transactions	0.23860	0.04697	325591
22	4	Cereals and preparations	0.24279	0.07713	372538
23	29	Crude animal, vegetable material	0.25210	0.07525	891959
24	5	Fruit and vegetables	0.26210	0.07729	7720982
25	33	Petroleum and products	0.27688	0.11227	575198
26	8	Animal feeding stuff	0.28996	0.09232	5028272
27	81	Plumbing, heating, lighting equipment	0.29046	0.13209	143621
28	57	Explosives & pyrotechnic products	0.29236	0.14484	55755
29	66	Nonmetal mineral manufactures,	0.30226	0.09167	125540
30	24	Wood, lumber & cork	0.30567	0.10155	1909359

Table 4.1 Continued

Rank	U.N. Code	Industry	Traditionality Index	Variance of Traditionality Index	Cumulative Real Exports 1991 U.S. $ (thousands)
31	73	Transport equipment	0.31440	0.08483	532502
32	41	Animal oils and fats	0.32802	0.09786	364213
33	25	Pulp and waste paper	0.33063	0.10895	2937119
34	51	Chemical elements & compounds	0.33238	0.08225	2071163
35	59	Chemicals, n.e.s.	0.33566	0.10945	84528
36	28	Metalliferous ores, scrap	0.33895	0.08536	13994807
37	0	Live animals	0.35216	0.07456	47724
38	67	Iron and steel	0.36496	0.16997	2386788
39	89	Misc. manufactured goods, n.e.s.	0.36499	0.10042	180766
40	71	Machinery, non-electric	0.37009	0.10516	326881
41	43	Processed animal, vegetable oil etc.	0.37740	0.14404	10201
42	72	Electrical machinery	0.37852	0.13728	291253
43	34	Gas-natural and manufactured	0.39632	0.24411	7826
44	69	Metal manufactures, n.e.s.	0.39798	0.21716	2448898
45	86	Instruments, watches, clocks	0.40450	0.06356	43643
46	64	Paper, paperboard and manufactures	0.41547	0.08718	1409986
47	6	Sugar and preparations, honey	0.41992	0.14114	212315
48	61	Leather, dressed; fur, etc.	0.42958	0.17242	32540
49	26	Textile fibers	0.43335	0.08102	491580
50	22	Oil seeds, nuts, kernels	0.44048	0.07785	13754
51	56	Fertilizers, manufactured	0.44283	0.09294	376449
52	96	Coin-nongold, noncurrent	0.47292	0.25568	16330
53	58	Plastic materials, etc.	0.48662	0.11634	285239
54	68	Non-ferrous metals	0.49435	0.08308	48403321
55	27	Crude fertilizers, minerals n.e.s.	0.51674	0.08044	1207221
56	21	Hides, skins & furs, undressed	0.54197	0.07703	110936
57	95	War-firearms, ammunition	0.55216	0.02287	16330

Table 4.2 Historical Data for 1963-1991

Year	GC	GEXP	GW	CSX	TRAD7	SPECL	RXR
1963	4.5	3.8	5.1	.94080	.	.59603	49.39
1964	3.8	9.1	6.6	.97036	.	.55982	72.22
1965	4.4	3.7	5.2	.97256	.033220	.54975	63.97
1966	7.0	24.9	5.6	.95524	.047433	.56655	58.70
1967	2.4	7.1	3.1	.92848	.023558	.58130	58.19
1968	3.4	1.3	4.4	.96728	.029327	.64501	51.87
1969	3.4	6.6	6.1	.95919	.028427	.62307	53.60
1970	3.8	4.8	5.1	.96737	.023046	.58110	52.88
1971	9.0	-17.7	3.8	.88777	.024534	.59803	59.23
1972	1.0	-11.5	4.2	.94366	.042297	.46570	65.37
1973	-4.9	22.4	5.7	.91037	.032818	.50276	52.93
1974	0.9	49	1.8	.92549	.016519	.62330	51.38
1975	-16.0	-31.3	1.0	.86095	.011092	.54456	37.57
1976	2.1	31.7	3.9	.94245	.010357	.43212	47.11
1977	8.6	-10.2	4.4	.89726	.025057	.39597	54.96
1978	7.5	9.5	4.9	.93688	.030124	.30983	54.56
1979	7.9	56.8	3.7	.87200	.024227	.29177	61.24
1980	4.7	-3.3	2.6	.90785	.017738	.36664	71.37
1981	4.5	-21.6	2.9	.88573	.025182	.33719	74.60
1982	-15.8	-9.2	0.5	.86627	.035696	.27395	61.61
1983	-1.5	4.1	3.3	.96328	.057854	.21718	48.91
1984	5.2	-6.6	5.0	.94196	.039553	.21777	43.96
1985	2.7	12	3.6	.88325	.018923	.20684	35.56
1986	2.1	8.3	3.8	.92723	.014644	.22979	35.06
1987	4.3	14.9	3.9	.89017	.0092597	.21064	35.61
1988	7.0	24.5	5.0	.93716	.0094490	.17933	36.67
1989	9.4	12.4	3.3	.93582	.	.18389	33.04
1990	8.9	3.5	2.5	.85239	.	.18220	34.5
1991	5.0	11.8	.	.92495	.	.20468	37.68

Chilean specialization index with respect to time. Note the high degree of specialization prior to 1971; this is essentially due to a high share of non-ferrous metals, primarily copper, in total exports. The index becomes volatile during the Allende years and begins a sustained decline from 1974 onward, with the structural adjustment being completed by 1988.

In the subsequent analysis, the three measures of export composition are compared to each other, to Chilean real GDP growth (GC), Chilean real export growth (GEXP), world real GDP growth (GW) and the real exchange rate (RXR). We also considered the rate of appreciation of the real exchange rate (DRXR), and the one-year lag of exchange rate appreciation. This last variable was included to capture possible J-curve effects. Table 4.2 illustrates the behavior of the main variables in the analysis. One can draw a broad picture of the relationship among growth, export structure, and macroeconomic variables over the 30-year period. In general, growth periods in Chile have been associated with upturns in the world business cycle and real exchange rate appreciation. The latter suggests that the value of the Chilean currency is driven primarily by domestic money demand (i.e. the degree of capital flight) rather than the exchange rate itself driving export performance. Growth periods are also associated with a stable composition of exports as measured by CSX and relative specialization as measured by SPECL. Recession periods, conversely, are associated with a structural change in exports, world recession, and exchange rate depreciation. This suggests that structural change in export composition is a response to crisis and is encouraged both by the change in relative prices associated with a devaluation and by the redeployment of unemployed assets during the recession period.

Looking at subperiods, a steady Chilean growth performance from 1962-1970 is associated with an increase in specialization, primarily an increased reliance on non-ferrous metals. The Allende years of 1971-1973 are associated with a sharp increase in diversification and are a focus of medium-run structural change. This is primarily due to the collapse of copper exports and the overvaluation of the exchange rate. After the one-shot rebound of copper in 1973-1974 (reflected in GEXP and SPECL), a long-run trend toward diversification sets in. However, the progress toward diversification is relatively smooth. The other large-scale episode of structural export change as measured by TRAD7 is centered on 1980-84. Unlike the episode of 1971-1973, which appears to be due to internal forces, the second episode is associated with the world growth slowdown and the onset of the Latin American debt crisis. But it shares with the first episode the association of rapid diversification and turnover of export industries with a crisis in export performance and the abrupt termination of a period of apparent overvaluation.

In pursuing our time-series analysis, we turned first to the question of Granger-Sims causality. As suggested above, our position is essentially that the interesting economic phenomenon labeled 'export-led growth' is something which manifests itself over an historical time frame, taking at least five years and perhaps decades. The Granger-Sims tests which have increasingly dominated the empirical literature on this subject are ill-suited for capturing such phenomena, as they measure only responses to short-run shocks with a year or two lag. Figure 4.3 illustrates cumulative experience functions for real GDP and exports for Chile over the period 1962-1991, analogous to the cumulative experience functions for specific export categories in Figure 4.1. It is apparent by inspection that output 'leads' exports over the relevant historical time frame. The rapid structural change in exports measured by SPECL and illustrated in Figure 4.2 corresponds to the time period virtually all observers would recognize as the Chilean experience of export dynamism. When Figure 4.3 is redone only for the period beginning in 1974, output continues to 'lead' exports. According to the philosophical notion underlying

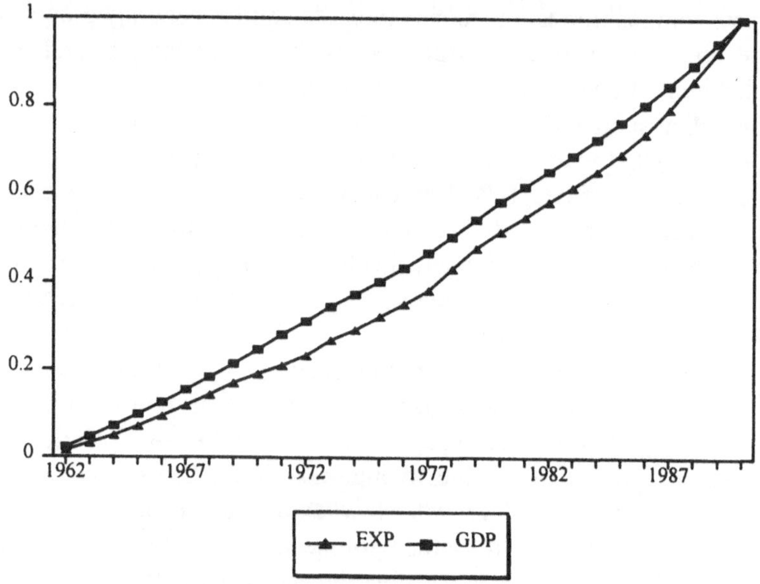

Figure 4.3 Cumulative Experience Functions

Granger-Sims tests, that export dynamism requires that exports precede output in time, Figure 4.3 stands as a sort of non-parametric test which rejects export-led growth in the Granger-Sims sense, even over a longer period of time.

The shorter time frame captured in an actual Granger-Sims test will be even less revealing of why exports were important to Chile; nonetheless, we present such a test. Initially we tested for the order of integration of the two series: exports (EXP) and gross domestic product (GDP). Both log (EXP) and log (GDP) were integrated of order one; therefore, both series needed to be first differenced before performing the Granger-Sims causality tests. Additionally we tested for cointegration to determine whether or not we would need to use error correction modeling (Bahmani-Oskooeeand Alse 1993). The series were not cointegrated; thus, the simple Granger-Sims tests were valid.[5] Of the variety of specifications of causality tests observed in the literature, one common one is as follows (cf. Serletis 1992):

$$\Delta\log(GDP) = \alpha_0 + \alpha(L)\Delta(GDP) + \beta(L)\Delta\log(EXP) + u_{1t}$$
$$\Delta\log(EXP) = \alpha_0 + \alpha(L)\Delta(GDP) + \beta(L)\Delta\log(EXP) + u_{2t}$$

where $\Delta\log(GDP)$ is the natural log of real Chilean gross domestic product first-differenced, $\Delta\log$ (EXP) is the natural log of real Chilean exports first-differenced, $\alpha(L)$ is a lag operator of the order 2, $\beta(L)$ is a lag operator of the order 2, and u_{1t}, u_{2t} are mean zero error terms. We carried out this test in growth rates of real Chilean GDP and real Chilean exports (GC and GEXP), effectively the same as log first differences, and employed two autoregressive lags. The autoregressive terms were not significant and are not reported. We obtained the following results (t-statistics in parentheses):

$$\underset{(1.33)}{GC = 2.11} + \underset{(1.16)}{0.26\,GC_{-1}} - \underset{(0.38)}{0.09\,GC_{-2}} + \underset{(0.05)}{0.003\,GEXP_{-1}} + \underset{(0.41)}{0.03\,GEXP_{-2}} \qquad R^2 = .08$$

$$\underset{(1.89)}{GEXP = 8.57} - \underset{(1.06)}{0.69\,GC_{-1}} + \underset{(1.87)}{1.24\,GC_{-2}} - \underset{(0.34)}{0.07\,GEXP_{-1}} - \underset{(1.43)}{0.29\,GEXP_{-2}} \qquad R^2 = .22$$

The second lag on output is marginally significant in the equation explaining exports, confirming the 'result' that there was no export-led growth in Chile and that output 'led' exports.

We wished also to see whether our three measures of export composition modified significantly the time-series macroeconomic relationships among Chilean output, Chilean exports, world output and exchange rates. In accordance with accepted practice in time-series econometrics, we performed Dickey-Fuller tests for stationarity in the variables of interest. CSX and GEXP are stationary, while GW, RXR, SPECL and TRAD7 are non-stationary at 5 percent but stationary after first-differencing; i.e. the log level of world output is stationary after second-differencing and the log level of Chilean exports is stationary after first-differencing. Applying a 5 percent level of significance creates a somewhat arbitrary dichotomy between GW and GC; the Dickey-Fuller test statistic is -3.402 for GW and -3.767 for GC. GC and GW are correlated both before and after first-differencing, so we followed the conservative procedure and first-differenced them both to guarantee stationarity (effectively second-differencing the log levels of both Chilean and world output). GEXP is uncorrelated with GW both before and after first-differencing, even at .2 significance. This is a bit surprising since one would expect on macroeconomic grounds that the transmission mechanism between GW and GC operates through GEXP. We decided to leave GEXP as it is since it is already stationary.

Carrying out the analysis on stationary variables, we then looked for reduced forms to explain Chilean aggregate growth and Chilean export growth. Chilean aggregate growth is fairly well tracked using world growth and real exchange rate fluctuations. Chilean real growth is positively correlated with appreciation of the real exchange rate, suggesting that the exchange rate is driven by domestic money demand. Upon seeking additional marginal effects of our export structure variables, we obtained the following (deltas indicate first-differenced variables, and t-statistics are in parentheses):

$$\Delta GC = \underset{(1.08)}{1.52} + \underset{(3.41)}{2.95}\,\Delta GW + \underset{(2.60)}{25.1}\,\Delta RXR + \underset{(1.96)}{48.3}\,\Delta SPECL \qquad R^2 = .50$$

$$\Delta GC = \underset{(1.52)}{-66.4} + \underset{(1.67)}{1.60}\,\Delta GW + \underset{(2.30)}{22.9}\,\Delta RXR + \underset{(1.54)}{72.9}\,CSX \qquad R^2 = .47$$

After controlling for world growth and exchange rates, Chilean growth is positively correlated with specialization at .10 using a two-tailed test. This reinforces the observation that the large moves toward export diversification have coincided with weak macroeconomic performance generally. Export diversification may represent a way of getting around a growth bottleneck associated with difficulties in marketing the current export mix, and the observed negative correlation thus reflects adjustment costs. The somewhat weaker result for CSX reinforces this finding. *Ceteris paribus*, Chilean growth is correlated with stability in the export mix relative to the previous year. The variable TRAD7 proved to be uncorrelated with Chilean growth after controlling for world growth and exchange rates, neither in first differences nor in levels.

The growth in Chilean exports is not highly correlated with world growth, as noted above; but it is negatively correlated with the lagged appreciation of the real exchange rate, as one might expect. After controlling for the real exchange rate, the impact of our export structure variables was as follows:

$$\underset{}{GEXP} = \underset{(3.95)}{288.4} - \underset{(3.83)}{70.3\,\Delta RXR_{-1}} + \underset{(1.96)}{113.5\,\Delta SPECL} \qquad R^2 = .47$$

$$\underset{}{GEXP} = \underset{(3.69)}{276.7} - \underset{(3.60)}{68.0\,\Delta RXR_{-1}} - \underset{(1.57)}{456.0\,\Delta TRAD7} \qquad R^2 = .44$$

The result for ΔSPECL confirms that in the equation for Chilean growth, reinforcing the likelihood that the adjustment costs of export diversification in terms of GDP growth operated at least in part through reduced export volumes. The result for TRAD7, while not quite significant at .10, is of the right sign and provides some additional robustness; medium-run structural change in exports is at least negatively correlated with export growth, *ceteris paribus*. The variable CSX proved not to be correlated with GEXP after controlling for lagged exchange rate appreciation.

Conclusion

There has been substantial export diversification in Chile since the mid-1970s, while little or no diversification took place before then. This suggests that such diversification was an important consequence of Chile's general program of economic liberalization. To some degree, liberalization and export diversification has been a response to economic crisis. While there has been a long-run trend toward diversification, the type of diversification observed is neither the emergence of heavy industries from protection suggested by the import-substitution model, nor the imitation of mature Northern manufactured products. The most striking source of diversification has been the emergence of new agricultural exports under the stimulus of real exchange rate depreciation.

In general, growth periods in Chile have been associated with upturns in the world business cycle, real exchange rate appreciation, and stability in the composition of exports, while recessionary periods have been associated with global recession, depreciation, and an acceleration of export diversification. Identifying the nature of this link between Chilean economic performance and export diversification represents the primary novel finding of this chapter. The direction of causation between growth and exchange rate appreciation is open to question. Although a long-run monetary model of the exchange rate fits the data, equally possible is the political willingness to relax the discipline of devaluation during good times, which may be common to all political regimes. Several observers have noted the disproportionate increase in consumer-goods imports in the 1980s, facilitated by overvaluation. The link between structural change in the export composition and weakness in GDP growth operates through a drop in export performance during times of structural change in exports, suggesting the existence of short-run adjustment costs to diversification.

These results are consistent with the possibility that in the long run, export diversification enhanced Chilean growth performance relative to what it would have been with a rigid export mix. Indeed, this seems likely. In order to test this hypothesis, long-run cross-country comparisons between countries which did and did not diversify would be useful. In addition, such an effort would reveal what, if any, relationships among export diversification, growth, and exchange rates are generalizable across countries, and which phenomena are country-specific. We believe this represents a fruitful area for future research.

Notes

1. An alternative, nonparametric method involves merging the data from the two industries to obtain a sample with $2(t_1 - t_0 + 1)$ observations on c_{it}. Then sort the data to take the lowest half of the observations. Under the null hypothesis, an equal number of these observations should have come from the two industries. Under the alternative hypothesis, a smaller number of the lowest $(t_1 - t_0 + 1)$ observations will have come from the more traditional industry; since its experience accumulates more rapidly, it has more high values. It can be shown that x, the number of observations in the lowest half of the combined sample coming from the more traditional industry, is distributed hypergeometrically. The above nonparametric test has the advantage of exploiting the exact distribution rather than the asymptotic properties of the sample mean, and it is also less sensitive to outliers; nonetheless, it is computationally expensive. We performed such tests on the 13 of export industries which ranked in the top 10 of two-digit industries either in 1962 or 1991, yielding 78 pairwise comparisons, and obtained very similar traditionality rankings as those obtained in Table 4.1, with a comparable number of rejections of the null hypothesis of equality of distributions. This reinforces our confidence that Table 4.1 provides a reasonable representation of the appropriate historical sequence.
2. This may well be due to technological change in the processing and transport of perishables. Anecdotal evidence suggests that advances in refrigeration and storage technology in recent years have made feasible the transport of such commodities as fruit and flowers over longer distances, and that some of this technology has been recently transferred from developed countries, e.g. Germany, to Chile. The existence of such technology transfer demonstrates that the 'product cycle' story can be an apt characterization of trade in agricultural as well as manufactured commodities. We are indebted to an anonymous referee for clarifying this point.
3. This is conceptually distinct from the within-industry variances presented in Table 4.1, which can be used to test for differences between industry means in traditionality.
4. An analogous measure for comparison of export structures across countries was originally proposed by Finger and Kreinin (1979); cf. Noland (1997) for an application to Asian countries.
5. Both series, log (EXP) and log (GDP), were integrated of order one as were the error terms of the cointegration equations. In order for the series to be cointegrated, the error terms of the simple Granger tests (the lag of the independent variable and the lag of the dependant variable are zero) would need to be integrated of order zero, thus requiring the use of error correction modeling. The Dickey-Fuller coefficients of the residuals of the cointegration equations were -3.212 and -3.032, respectively. There is a failure to reject the hypothesis of an unit root at the 5 percent significance level. Given that log(exp) and

log(gdp) are not cointegrated we are able to perform simple Granger-Sims tests (Bahmani-Oskooee and Alse 1993).

References

Amin Gutiérrez de Piñeres, S. (1996), 'Externalities in the Export Sector and Long Run Growth Rates', *Singapore Economic Review*, vol. 41, no. 1 (April), pp. 13-24.

Bahmani-Oskooee, M., and J. Alse (1993), 'Export Growth and Economic Growth: An Application of Cointegration and Error Correction Modeling', *Journal of Developing Areas*, vol. 27 (July), pp.535-542.

Bahmani-Oskooee, M., M. Hamid and S. Ghiath (1991), 'Exports, growth and causality in LDCs: A Re-examination', *Journal of Development Economics*, vol. 36 , no.2, pp. 405-415.

Balassa, B. (1978), 'Exports and Economic Growth: Further Evidence', *Journal of Development Economics*', vol. 5, no. 2, pp. 181-89.

Behrman, J. (1976), *Foreign Trade Regimes and Economic Development: Chile*, New York: National Bureau of Economic Research.

Dollar, D. (1986), 'Technological Innovation, Capital Mobility and the Product Cycle in North-South Trade', *American Economic Review*, vol 76 no. 1, pp. 177-190.

Edwards, S. and A. Edwards (1987), *Monetarism and Liberalization: The Chilean Experiment,* Cambridge, Mass.: Ballinger.

Edwards, S. (1993), 'Openness, Trade Liberalization, and Growth in Developing Countries', *Journal of Economic Literature*, vol. 31, pp. 1358-1393.

Emery, R. (1967), The Relation of Exports and Economic Growth, *Kyklos*, vol. 20, no. 4, pp. 470-84.

Esfahani, H. (1991), 'Exports, Imports, and Economic Growth in Semi-industrialized Countries', *Journal of Development Economics*, vol. 35 no. 1, pp. 93-116.

Finger, J.M. and M. Kreinin (1979), 'A Measure of "Export Similarity" and its Possible Uses', *Economic Journal*, vol. 89, pp. 905-12.

Foxley, A. (1983), *Latin American Experiments in Neo-Conservative Economics*, Berkeley: University of California Press.

Grossman, G. and E. Helpman (1991), *Innovation and Growth in the Global Economy,* Cambridge, Mass.: MIT Press.

Helpman, E. and P. Krugman (1985), *Market Structure and Foreign Trade*, Cambridge, Mass.: MIT Press.

Jung, W. and P. Marshall (1985), 'Exports, Growth and Causality in Developing Countries', *Journal of Development Economics*, vol. 18 no. 2, pp. 1-12.

Kravis, I. (1970), 'Trade as a Handmaiden of Growth', *Economic Journal*, vol. 80, no. 320, pp. 850-72.

Krueger, A. (1978), *Foreign Trade Regimes and Economic Development: Liberalization Attempts and Consequences,* Cambridge, MA: Ballinger Pub. Co. for NBER.

Krugman, P. (1979), 'A Model of Innovation, Technology Transfer and the World

Distribution of Income', *Journal of Political Economy,* vol. 87, pp. 253-266.

Krugman, P. (1981), 'Intraindustry Specialization and the Gains from Trade', *Journal of Political Economy,* vol. 89, pp.959-973.

Markusen, J. (1986), 'Explaining the Volume of Trade', *American Economic Review*, vol. 76, no. 5, pp. 1002-1011.

Michaely, M. (1977), 'Exports and Growth: An Empirical Investigation', *Journal of Development Economics*, vol. 4, no. 1. Pp. 49-53.

Moschos, D. (1989), 'Export Expansion, Growth and the Level of Economic Development', *Journal of Development Economics*, vol. 30, pp. 93-102.

Noland, Marcus (1997), 'Has Asian Export Performance Been Unique?', *Journal of International Economics*, vol. 43, no. ½ (August), pp. 79-102.

Prebisch, R. (1950), *The Economic Development of Latin America and its Principal Problems,* NY: United Nations.

Rosenstein-Rodan, P. (1943), 'Problems of Industrialization of Eastern and South-Eastern Europe', *The Economic Journal*, vol. 53, pp. 202-211.

Segerstrom, P., T. Anant and E. Dinopolous (1990), 'A Schumpeterian Model of the Product Life Cycle', *American Economic Review*, vol. 80, pp. 1077-1092.

Serletis, A. (1992), 'Export Growth and Canadian Economic Development', *Journal of Development Economics*, vol. 38, no. 1, pp.133-45.

Singer, H. (1952), 'The Mechanics of Economic Development', *The Indian Economic Review*.

Singer, H. (1950), 'The Distribution of Gains Between Investing and Borrowing Countries', *American Economic Review*, vol. 40 no. 2, pp. 473-85.

Summers, R. and A. Heston (1988), 'The Penn World Table (Mark 5): An Expanded Set of International Comparisons, 1950-1988', *Quarterly Journal of Economics*, vol. 106, no. 2, pp. 327-368.

Vernon, R. (1966), 'International Investment and International Trade in the Product Cycle', *Quarterly Journal of Economics*, vol. 80, pp. 190-207.

5 Export Sector Dynamics and Domestic Growth: The case of Colombia*

Introduction

It is well known that for a number of developing countries, export growth appears to 'cause' economic growth.[1] The finding that short-run bursts in export growth precede acceleration in economic growth is often advanced as evidence in favor of outward-oriented policies, whether of the non-discriminatory or overtly export-promoting type. Elsewhere (Amin and Ferrantino, 1997) we have argued that this is not a particularly productive way to look at the relationship between exports and growth - long-run economic success requires sustained commitment to appropriate policies, and long-run effects are not well captured by findings of 'causation' over periods of a year or two. In the case of Chile, for example, export diversification rather than exporting *per se* turns out to be more important in understanding Chilean economic performance under reform.

Another difficulty with interpreting the evidence of 'causation' between developing-country exports and growth is that the empirical results differ substantially across countries (for a broad review of the literature see Edwards, 1993). Colombia is one country for which the data do not support the conventional hypothesis of export-led growth.[2] A number of reasons can be advanced for this. The short-run growth benefits of exporting may come largely by relaxation of the foreign exchange constraint, facilitating the growth of imported inputs (Esfahani, 1991). Colombia did not experience the severe foreign exchange difficulties of many other Latin American countries, minimizing the importance of the foreign exchange constraint as a channel

---

* This chapter is reprinted with some revisions by the authors from Amin Gutiérrez de Piñeres, Sheila and Michael J. Ferrantino, 'Export Sector Dynamics and Economic Growth: The Case of Colombia', *Review of Development Economics*, October 1999, vol. 3, no.3, pp. 268-280.

linking exports to growth. Another possibility is that growth in primary-product exports (either coffee, illicit drugs, or both) may have drawn excessive resources from other sectors, leading to 'Dutch-disease' effects on aggregate growth. Given the above possibilities, should one then believe that export performance is irrelevant for Colombia, or that Colombia can implement distortionary inward-oriented policies costlessly? Probably not; but the evidence does suggest digging deeper for the relationship between export performance and growth performance.

We begin by presenting the theoretical motivation which allows us the capture the dynamics in the export sector and its impact on growth. Next, we replicate the widespread rejection of the conventional export-led growth hypothesis for Colombia. To develop an empirical model that integrates this concept of structural change in the export sector as a key source of growth we generate several measures of export diversification and structural change in exports. Our results indicate that increased export diversification leads to more rapid growth in real exports; and, that more rapid structural change in exports is associated with accelerated growth in Colombian GDP. Additionally, new (for Colombia) primary products, such as coal, flowers, and fish, can serve as 'non-traditional' export sectors just as well as can manufactures.

Theoretical Motivation

The hypothesis we seek to test is that exports may affect aggregate growth through externalities or spillovers from one export sector to another. This idea can be motivated using a three-sector model with two export sectors and an import-competing sector. The equilibrium solution of such a model is derived in Amin Gutiérrez de Piñeres (1997).

The Latin American experience demonstrates that knowledge gained by exporting goods produced in sector one can be utilized by other exporters. This knowledge may range from simple diffusion of awareness of export opportunities to dissemination of transport and refrigeration technologies to expansion of the domestic services base in insurance, merchant banking, etc., required to handle export transactions. For example, in Chile, a variety of fresh fruits were exported subsequent to the export success of table grapes. In Colombia, fresh cut flowers were followed by other highly perishable produce.

The model assumes a knowledge spillover between export sectors, linked to the utilization of human capital in one of the export sectors. This means equilibrium growth is increasing in the share of output allocated to the externality-generating export sector. The presence of the externality thus insures that the model exhibits endogenous growth behavior. Since the spillover increases returns to production in the other export sector as well, higher growth rates are associated with a higher export/GDP ratio in the aggregate. Since we do not know *a priori* which export commodities exhibit greater externalities, we hypothesize that episodes during which the structural composition of exports is changing rapidly or during which export diversification is increasing may signal increases in the output of the externality-generating sectors. This auxiliary hypothesis forms the bridge between the theoretical structure and the empirical exercise presented below.

Historical Overview of the Colombian Economy

Useful and detailed surveys of Colombian development at various phases of the process are provided by Garcia Garcia and Montes Llamas (1988), Hallberg (1991) and Cohen and Gunter (1992). For the present purpose, we need to emphasize several salient facts. The first is a pattern of relatively high long run growth punctuated by crisis. Prior to 1966, the Colombian economy was characterized by high inflation. Beginning in 1966, favorable world economic conditions and moderate fiscal and monetary policies stimulated overall growth. During the coffee bonanza (1975-1982) government spending increased dramatically as economic growth decelerated. From 1966 until 1974, annual growth rates of real GDP averaged 6.57 percent, while during the coffee bonanza real GDP growth decelerated to 4.05 percent annually. Since 1983, annual growth rates of GDP have averaged only 3.3 percent as coffee prices have gradually eased.

The long-run growth performance described above took place under the background of a wide variety of policy experiments. From 1950-1966 the Colombian economy was characterized by import substitution policies and a fixed exchange rate. During this period, the country faced a time of rural unrest, known as 'La Violencia'. In August of 1966, President Lleras Restrepo took office. Lleras began a program of austerity that included trade and exchange rate controls, tight credit policies, tax reforms, a balanced budget, and an emphasis on export expansion and import substitution (Worldmark, 1984). During this period the Colombian economy showed stable and consistent growth, aided by favorable world economic conditions.

Policies of export promotion and import substitution were reversed in 1975 (Garcia Garcia and Montes Llamas, 1988). The first 'coffee bonanza' period was characterized by sharply rising coffee prices during 1976-1977, with exports following with about a two-year lag. The boom in export revenues concealed a number of policy mistakes, such as unsustainable growth of government expenditures. Subsequently, the debt crisis of 1982-1983 resulted in the need for a macroeconomic stabilization program in 1984. The stabilization program of 1984 included a drastic reduction in the fiscal deficit and the devaluation of the Colombian peso. While, there was a modest liberalization inward orientation of the trade regime was not fundamentally altered. During 1986-1987 there was a small coffee bonanza. Faced with falling coffee prices in 1988, the government was forced to enact a serious stabilization program.

In 1990, the Colombian government embarked on a massive liberalization program. The commitment to liberalization began in the late 1980s under President Barco's administration and was further supported in the early 1990s under the administration of President Gaviria. The trade liberalization program eliminated most nontariff barriers and dramatically reduced tariffs. The government also implemented a program of financial liberalization, eliminating the previous system of exchange rate controls and permitting free flows of foreign exchange and international capital. To make Colombia more attractive to foreign investment, restrictions of direct foreign investment were reduced and labor laws rewritten to provide for increased flexibility in hiring and firing.

Data and Analysis

Basic Data

Two-digit SITC export data from the United Nations trade database for the years 1962-1993 were used to derive empirical measures of the 'traditionality' of specific export industries, described below, as well as measures of the degree of export diversification and structural change taking place in Colombia's export portfolio. Nominal export values were deflated by appropriate product specific price deflators. Primary commodities were deflated commodity price indices from the United Nations *Monthly Bulletin of Statistics* and IMF *International Financial Statistics*. Manufactures were deflated by their appropriate U.S. producer price index, using the general U.S. producer price index when an industry-level one was not available. In the regression analysis we use the following variables: the growth rate of real Colombian GDP (GC), from the International Comparisons Project (Summers and Heston, 1991); world growth rates (GW), derived from IMF-IFS data; real Colombian exports (GEXP), as aggregated from our deflated two-digit SITC data; the Colombian real effective export exchange rate (REXP)[3] and subsidy rates for Colombian exports (SUBSIDY) are from Ocampo and Villar (1994); and world interest rates (GI) are the yearly high for U.S. corporate bond rates (Taylor, 1997) which are used as a proxy for borrowing rates. The values for these variables are presented in Table 5.1. We calculate the value of imported intermediate inputs (IMP) in much the same way as in Esfahani (1991). The variable IMP is composed of the value of imports of crude materials, mineral fuels, animal/vegetable oil and fats, chemicals less pharmaceuticals and perfumes/cosmetics, basic manufactures, and machinery/transport equipment less road vehicles and planes. The price of coffee (DCOFFEE) and oil (DOIL) are the U.N. commodity price index for Colombian coffee and for oil, respectively.

Measures of Export Specialization and Structural Change

As a first step, we calculated a cumulative export experience function for each commodity. This is obtained as

$$c_{it} = \sum_{i,t_0}^{t} e_{it} / \sum_{i,t_0}^{t_1} e_{it}$$

where t_0 and t_1 represent the initial and terminal periods of the sample, in this case 1962 and 1993. Additionally, let e_{it} represent exports by Colombian

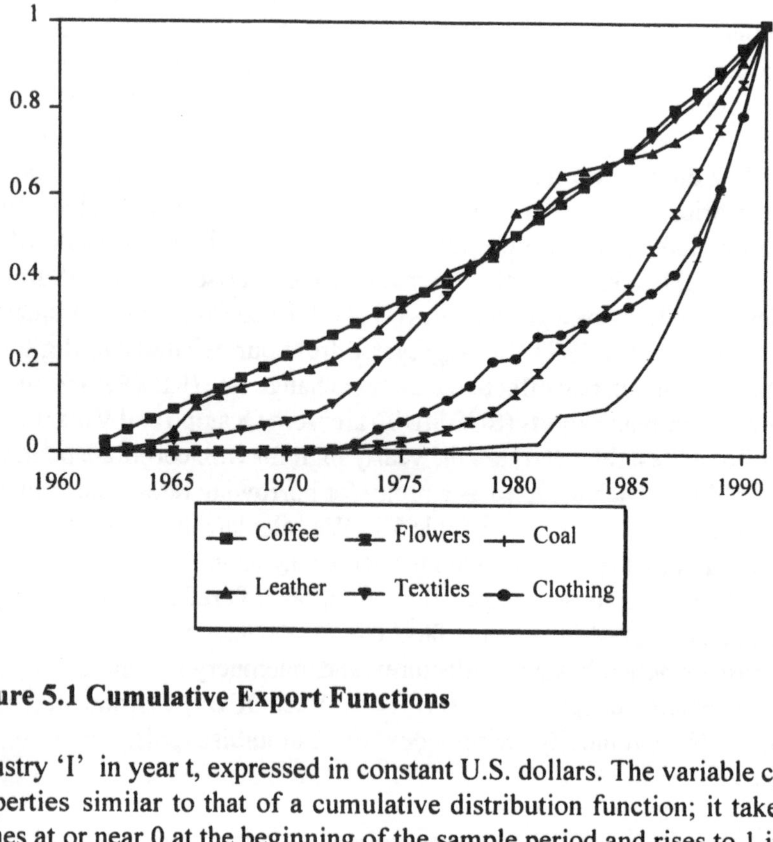

Figure 5.1 Cumulative Export Functions

industry 'I' in year t, expressed in constant U.S. dollars. The variable c_{it} has properties similar to that of a cumulative distribution function; it takes on values at or near 0 at the beginning of the sample period and rises to 1 in the final year. If values of c_{it} for two different industries are plotted together, an industry whose export experience was concentrated earlier in the period (a 'traditional' industry) can be distinguished from an industry whose export experience was concentrated later in the period (a 'non-traditional' industry) because its export experience function would be shifted to the left.

Cumulative export experience functions for some important Colombian export commodities are displayed in Figure 5.1. Such functions can be used to obtain a visual representation of the movement from traditional to non-traditional exports, in this case from coffee to textiles to clothing and flowers (with clothing exports accelerating relative to flower exports later in the

Table 5.1 Historical Data for 1963-1993

Year	GC	GEXP	GW	GI	REXR	wtTRAD7	SPECL	DSUBSIDY
1963	3.6	2.27	5.1	4.37	.	.	.44544	
1964	8.2	5.46	6.6	4.45	.	.	.43772	
1965	.75	3.21	5.2	4.73	.	0.00003237	.42843	
1966	9.0	-9.66	5.6	5.52	.	0.00003806	.39227	
1967	.42	2.69	3.1	6.24	82.9	0.00002689	.38717	23.1
1968	7.7	-1.64	4.4	6.53	90.1	0.00002874	.38316	21.2
1969	6.6	11.93	6.1	7.84	90.3	0.00005197	.37594	19.1
1970	8.9	6.51	5.1	8.60	95.7	0.00005445	.33658	19.8
1971	7.7	-5.08	3.8	7.71	103.9	0.00008705	.34571	22.6
1972	5.9	2.47	4.2	7.36	111.3	0.00012159	.31814	26.8
1973	7.2	8.34	5.7	7.77	109.2	0.00013605	.26409	26.6
1974	5.7	-8.94	1.8	9.38	104.6	0.00010121	.24207	23.5
1975	.8	-1.01	1.0	9.01	100.0	0.00008331	.24266	13.0
1976	5.6	-16.65	3.9	8.65	93.0	0.00008404	.25996	10.2
1977	4.5	9.72	4.4	8.30	83.4	0.00007827	.21381	9.9
1978	7.9	34.71	4.9	9.28	86.3	0.00009170	.18756	14.1
1979	4.7	1.01	3.7	10.91	82.5	0.00004274	.28301	14.1
1980	4.7	15.32	2.6	13.59	85.0	0.00003452	.28792	15.1
1981	3.0	-9.41	2.9	15.96	84.0	0.00003363	.31114	16.4
1982	1.6	-.961	0.5	15.48	79.5	0.00006536	.28437	18.8
1983	.85	1.27	3.3	12.79	80.5	0.00011250	.28522	23.7
1984	2.7	2.91	5.0	13.75	89.8	0.00012209	.30717	27.0
1985	.33	6.82	3.6	12.69	102.2	0.00010048	.32866	26.4
1986	5.9	37.96	3.8	10.26	113.6	0.00008846	.28646	18.4
1987	4.8	29.68	3.9	11.06	113.7	0.00007680	.26531	15.6
1988	2.8	-5.07	5.0	10.18	112.3	0.00004393	.24147	14.1
1989	3.4	15.07	3.3	9.90	115.3	0.00002512	.20563	14.8
1990	4.1	11.39	2.5	9.68	127.2	0.00003744	.21175	12.8
1991	2.3	11.99	0.8	9.12	121.1	.	.15917	10.6
1992	4.2	4.53	1.3	8.39	112.2	.	.18409	7.9
1993	5.3	1.1	1.8	7.99		.	.18409	

period) to coal. Note that there is no necessary association of traditionality with primary products and nontraditionality with manufactures. In the Colombian context, coffee is traditional and coal is nontraditional on a pure reading of the data. As noted above, primary product sectors as well as manufacturing can give rise to the type of learning-by-doing effects and knowledge spillovers conducive to growth (Amin Gutiérrez de Piñeres, 1996).

The traditionality index is constructed as the mean of the cumulative export experience index for each industry as

$$T_i = \sum_{t=t_0}^{t_1} c_{it}/(t_1 - t_0 + 1)$$

Here, more traditional industries would have a higher score for T_i. we calculate traditionality scores T_i for the full set of 52 two-digit export industries. A sample of these are presented in Table 5.2. It is easy again to reject the null hypothesis that all exports followed the same pattern of historical growth. For example, 'flowers', the 9th least traditional industry, is less traditional than 'coffee', the 44th least traditional industry, at standard levels of significance. Strictly speaking, such hypothesis tests are not particularly informative since the traditionality index simply represents a characterization of the actual universe of data, rather than a small sample from some imaginary large sample of alternate Colombian export histories. Nonetheless, it is clear enough that Colombia has been actively exporting some types of goods for a long time and others only recently.

Parts of the Colombian story, such as the shift from reliance on coffee and sugar toward flowers and clothing, can be readily identified in Table 5.2. The table reinforces the point that it is a mistake to identify primary products with 'traditionality' and manufacturing with 'non-traditionality', or to assume that a country exporting more manufactures is evolving in the direction of its true comparative advantage. In Colombia, primary products industries including flowers, fruits, fish, and dairy products are among the newest successful exporters. Furniture, manufactures of metals, non-metallic mineral manufactures are relatively 'traditional' when the historical record is examined. The manufactures clearly belong to the earlier regime of export promotion/ import substitution, and have proved to be unsustainable on the basis of costs.

We generated two measures of the composition of exports, which capture medium-run structural change and static specialization/diversification,

Table 5.2 Temporal Sequencing of Colombian Real Exports 1962-1993
(Nontraditional exports first)

Rank	Industry	Traditionality Index	Variance of Traditionality	Cumulative Real Exports (1993) (millions of U.S. dollars)
1	Processed animal, vegetable oils	0.03125	0.03125	94
2	Fixed vegetable oil and fat	0.0625	0.06048	4158
3	Dairy products	0.06513	0.04833	9459
4	Explosives	0.06723	0.03687	255596
5	Beverages	0.13291	0.06244	65032
6	Coal,coke	0.13662	0.07307	3672980
7	Metalliferous ores and scraps	0.17243	0.05812	35871
8	Clothing	0.2013	0.07073	3378886
9	Crude animal products (flowers)	0.2027	0.08023	3693301
10	Fish and preparations	0.20908	0.06595	925614
23	Perfume,cleaning products	0.32655	0.10202	114934
24	Electrical machinery	0.32949	0.10604	473476
25	Nonmetal mineral manufactures	0.33956	0.07757	3125856
26	Cereals and preparations	0.34312	0.10612	342537
27	plumbing ,heating and lighting	0.35148	0.11705	157673
28	Oilseeds, nuts and kernels	0.35535	0.08797	50888
29	Fertilizer manufactures	0.3554	0.09843	51330
30	Metal manufactures	0.36067	0.09844	798763
44	Coffee, tea and spices	0.4245	0.08111	51023656
45	Non-ferrous metals	0.45181	0.1023	226827
46	Tobacco and manufactures	0.4642	0.08814	854539
47	Textile fibres	0.48718	0.10258	1738102
48	Meat and preparations	0.5021	0.13779	541640
49	Live animals	0.59847	0.12012	340898
50	Animal feeding stuff	0.71533	0.12857	113774
51	Wood, lumber	0.73708	0.09271	154639
52	Hides, skins	0.7743	0.10451	77818

respectively. The first measure, TRAD7, is the variance of traditionality scores using seven-year intervals rather than the full sample period. Thus, we have values of TRAD7 for 1965-1990; the value for 1965, e.g. is the variance of the 52 industry values of T_i obtained using the period 1962-1968 as a reference period. When the variance is high, this implies that the industries experienced relatively divergent patterns of export growth during the period, with some being leaders and some laggers, so that a high variance is interpreted as an episode of structural change centered on the period in question. A low variance implies that the composition of exports was relatively stable over the 7-year period. Given that Colombia has a few exports that command a larger share of its export portfolio we also constructed a weighted TRAD7 index (WTRAD7). WTRAD7 weighs each traditionality score by the real export share of that industry for that specific year, then calculates the variance. This allows us to capture the influence of the predominant export sectors, such as oil and coffee, on the TRAD7 index.[4] The weighted index is used in the subsequent regression analysis and the values are reported in Table 5.1. Visually, a high value of WTRAD7 corresponds to a large dispersion among curves of the type shown in Figure 5.2, and vice versa. The years from 1973-80 exhibit accelerated structural change, corresponding to the two oil shocks and the coffee bonanza. A second period of structural change comes in 1983-87, which includes the 1984 stabilization and the second coffee bonanza.

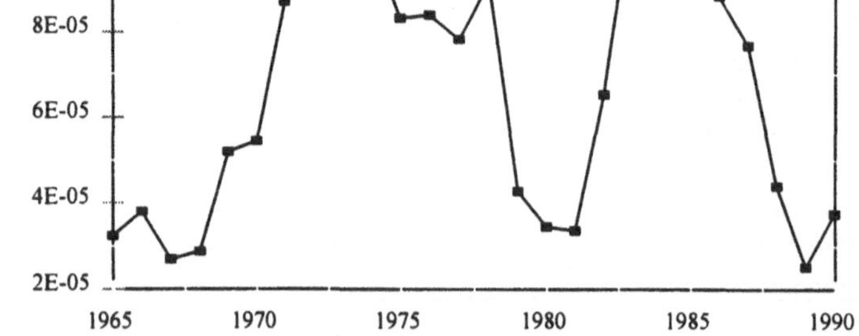

Figure 5.2 Weighted TRAD7

A static measure of specialization, SPECL, is calculated as:

$$SPECL_t = \sum_{i=1}^{54} (s_{i,t})^2$$

where $s_{it} = e_{it} / \sum_{I \in (1,54)} e_{it}$, the share of industry I's exports in national exports in year t. A score approaching 1 implies reliance on a single export (a high degree of specialization) while a score approaching 0 implies a high degree of export diversification. The behavior of SPECL is illustrated in Figure 5.3. There is a long-run trend toward export diversification, which is temporarily reversed in 1979-1985 (toward the end of the first coffee boom) but resumes in 1986. Table 5.1 summarizes the performance of the export structure variables. A steady Colombian growth performance from 1966-1974 is associated with an decrease in specialization. The coffee bonanza years are associated with a sharp decrease in diversification (increase in specialization) from 1978-1981. During the debt crisis years of 1982-1983, the move towards

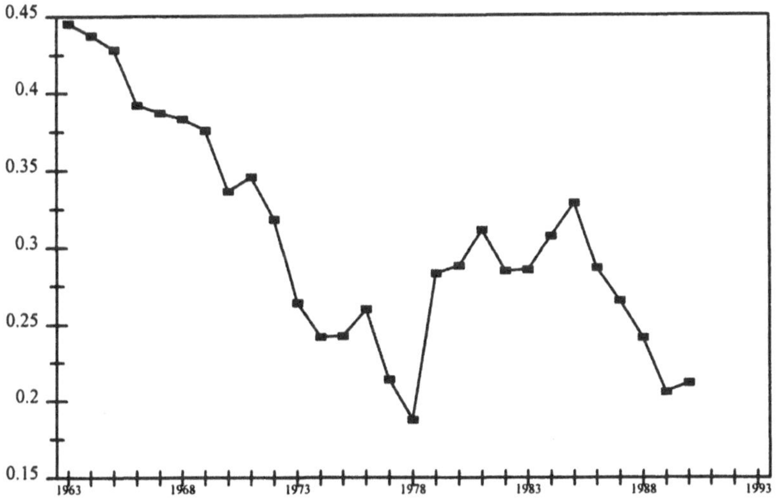

Figure 5.3 SPECL Index

diversification resumes. While Colombia did not experience the deep recession that hit other Latin American economies at this time, its growth performance did decelerate, and during 1981-1982 real export volumes declined. The trend toward diversification of exports is sustained through the end of the sample, with a modest reversal associated with the little coffee boom (1983-1985).

Relationship between Exports and Output

Tests for the short-run relationship between Colombian exports and GDP were performed using the methodology of cointegration and error-correction modeling (Bahmani-Oskooee and Alse, 1993). In the following discussion, the letter 'D' preceding a variable name denotes its first-differenced value throughout, while the number '1' following a variable name denotes its one-year lagged value. The time series LEXP (natural log real exports) and LGDP (natural log real GDP) are I(1); that is, they are stationary in first differences.[5] For the variables LEXP and LGDP to be cointegrated, the error terms in the regressions of LEXP on LGDP and of LGDP on LEXP must both be I(0); that is, they must themselves be stationary. The hypothesis of cointegration of LEXP and LGDP is strongly rejected by the data (see endnote 5). Thus, it is appropriate to perform standard Granger-Sims causality tests on the first differences of the two variables, i.e. on their growth rates (cf. Serletis, 1992):[6]

$$\text{DLEXP} = f(\text{DLEXP1, DLGDP1}) \qquad (1)$$
$$\text{DLGDP} = g(\text{DLEXP1, DLGDP1}) \qquad (2)$$

The results are reported in Table 5.3. We do not find strong evidence for export-led growth in the Granger sense. Yet, the question remains in what manner exports could affect growth. Another possible channel through which exports may affect domestic growth is by reducing foreign exchange constraints. Easing of the constraint should facilitate the purchase of intermediate inputs and relieve bottlenecks in the production process (Esfahani, 1991). We expanded equations 1 and 2 to include current and lagged values of the natural log of the imported intermediate inputs (LIMP) in Colombia. The general regression model is as follows and the results are reported in Table 5.3:

DLEXP = f(DLEXP1, DLGDP1, DLIMP, DLIMP1) (3)
DLGDP = g(DLEXP1, DLGDP1, DLIMP, DLIMP1) (4)

All variables remain insignificant. Thus, we did not find any evidence for a role of foreign exchange constraints in the Colombian case. It should be noted that the large inflows of U.S. dollars from the illegal drug industry has alleviated the foreign exchange constraint to an extent perhaps not fully reflected in official statistics. At a rough estimate, between 1 and 4 billion U.S. dollars are generated annually by the illegal drug sector in Colombia (Thoumi, 1995, Table 6.1). Unfortunately, the lack of reliable data on the value of the illegal drug trade and the amount of capital inflows from this activity make it impossible to include illegal drug exports in the analysis. However, the question still remains is there a manner in which the export sector affects the growth rate of an economy. We propose to answer that question by studying the impact of the structural change and diversification in the export sector and its impact on domestic and export growth rates.

Relationship Among Export Structural Change, Exports, and Output

In order to move beyond simple tests of Granger causality we attempted to include our variables that characterize the dynamics of the export sector in the models that explain export and GDP growth rates.[7] The system of equations estimated is as follows:[8]

DLGDP = f(DLIMP, DWTRAD7, DLEXP1, DLGW1, DCOFFEE) (5)
DLEXP = g(DCOFFEE, DGI, DREXP) (6)
DWTRAD7 = h(DLEXP1, DLGW1, DSUBSIDY, DOIL, DLGDP) (7)
DSPECL = j(DGI, DREXP, DWTRAD71) (8)
DLIMP = k(DLIMP1, DLGW) (9)

The results are reported in Table 5.4a-b. Each equation was estimated by OLS, and the system was estimated using three-stage least squares (3SLS). The system is reported as equations 10-14 in Table 5.4a-b. The principal features of the system are robust to the manner in which simultaneity is handled.

Table 5.3 Causality Tests (standard errors in parentheses)

	Dependent variable			
Independent variables	1 DLGDP	2 DLEXP	3 DLGDP	4 DLEXP
INTERCEPT	.0355*** (.010)	.0680 (.053)	.0310*** (.0104)	.0533 (.0560)
LGDP1	.139 (.199)	-.453 (1.020)	.225 (.205)	-.0902 (1.10)
LEXP1	.0424 (.0412)	.127 (.211)	.0504 (.0403)	.146 (.217)
LIMP			.0207 (.0181)	.0256 (.0976)
LIMP1			-.0115 (.0185)	-.0751 (.0994)
N	24	24	24	24
R^2	.08	.02	.21	.08

***- significant at .01. No other variables significant at .10 or better.

The GDP growth equation (eq. 5 and 10) indicates that Colombian growth is stimulated by high world growth, high coffee prices, and increased structural change in Colombian exports. As seen above, increased structural change takes place during periods of higher coffee prices, implying that Colombia has successfully utilized coffee revenues to finance a program of diversification. Lagged export growth has both a direct and indirect effect on current GDP growth. The direct effect as measured through the GDP equation is significant and positive. On the other hand, accelerated export growth is associated with a decrease in structural change in the equation for change in traditionality (equations 7 and 12), and thus indirectly with decreased Colombian growth.

Table 5.4a Structural Regressions (standard errors in parentheses)

	OLS Dependent variables				
Independent variables	5 DLGDP	6 DLEXP	7 DWTRAD7	8 DSPECL	9 DLIMP
INTERCEPT	-.00697 (.00936)	.0365 (.0257)	1.90E-5** (8.58E-6)	-.00934 (.00735)	.284* (.158)
DLIMP	.00490 (.0103)				
DWTRAD7	488.0*** (150.3)				
DLEXP1	.0654** (.0282)		-9.18E-5*** (2.52E-5)		
DLGW1	1.31*** (.237)		-.00117*** (.00030)		
DCOFFEE	4.98E-6*** (1.72E-6)	-.0310 (.0201)			
DGI		.0230 (.0191)		.00617 (.00603)	
DREXP		.00796* (.00397)		.000500 (.00116)	
DSUBSIDY			2.85E-6*** (8.6E-7)		
DOIL			-2.85E-6*** (8.6E-7)		
DLIMP1					-.543*** (.173)
DLGDP			.000672*** (.000184)		
DWTRAD71				-.00667 (.00644)	
DLGW					-6.14 (4.03)
N	24	24	24	24	24
R^2	.72	.19	.71	.05	.35

* - significant at .10 ** - significant at .05 *** - significant at .01

Table 5.4b Structural Regressions (standard errors in parentheses)

	3SLS Dependent variables				
Independent variables	10 DLGDP	11 DLEXP	12 DWTRAD7	13 DSPECL	14 DLIMP
INTERCEPT	-.00531	.0356	1.89E-5**	-.00996	.352***
	(.00953)	(.0257)	(8.59E-6)	(.00717)	(.127)
DLIMP	-.000596				
	(.0125)				
DWTRAD7	476.4**				
	(165.7)				
DLEXP1	.0663**		-.000102***		
	(.0302)		(2.56E-5)		
DLGW1	1.27***		-.00171***		
	(.239)		(.000390)		
DCOFFEE	5.01E-6***	-.0314			
	(1.84E-6)	(.0198)			
DGI		.0229		.0106**	
		(.0187)		(.00496)	
DREXP		.00842**		.000812	
		(.00392)		(.000952)	
DSUBSIDY			2.02E-6**		
			(7.76E-7)		
DOIL			-.2.02E-6**		
			(7.75E-7)		
DLIMP1					-.469***
					(.135)
DLGDP			.00112**		
			(.000294)		
DWTRAD71				-.0114**	
				(.00532)	
DLGW					-8.10**
					(3.12)
N	System Weighted MSE 1.37 with 97 degrees of freedom				
R^2	System Weighted R^2 .54				

* - significant at .10 ** - significant at .05 *** - significant at .01

The reduced-form coefficient for the effect of export growth on GDP growth may be calculated as:

$$dDLGDP/dDLEXP1=\partial DLGDP/\partial DLEXP1+ (\partial DLGDP/\partial DWTRAD7)(\partial DWTRAD7/\partial DLEXP1) \qquad (15)$$

The reduced-form coefficient comes to .0206 with a standard error of .0337 in the OLS system, yielding a t-statistic of 0.61. The corresponding measure in 3SLS is .0177 with a standard error of .0367, giving a t-statistic of 0.48. Thus, the total effect of export growth on GDP growth is weakly positive but does not achieve statistical significance. The low value of the coefficient (a 1 percent increase in export growth leads to only a .02 percent increase in GDP growth) implies that export growth largely crowds out non-export growth, but the lack of statistical significance precludes any strong conclusions about the presence or absence of Dutch-disease phenomena.

In the export equation (equations 6 and 11), export growth accelerates with exchange rate depreciation, as is to be expected, and is marginally negatively associated with higher coffee prices, implying that there is some crowding-out of other exports by coffee exports. Other determinants of structural change (equations 7 and 12), in addition to falling exports, are a deceleration in world GDP growth, an increase in Colombian GDP growth (implying two-way influence between Colombian growth and structural change), an increase in export subsidies and falling oil prices. The acceleration of export structural change during adverse global macroeconomic conditions has also been observed for Chile (Amin Gutiérrez de Piñeres and Ferrantino, 1997). This suggests that exporters respond to adversity in a Schumpeterian fashion, reacting to the destruction of former opportunities with an intensified effort to create new opportunities.

The long-run increase in overall export diversification for Colombia, documented above, appears neither to accelerate or decelerate with respect to any of the variables analyzed, nor does export specialization emerge as a determinant of Colombian export growth or Colombian GDP growth, as it is excluded from these equations by the Akaike Information Criterion. The growth rate of imported intermediate inputs is primarily a mean-reverting process (the coefficient on its lagged value is negative). Like specialization, the rate of importation of intermediates appears to be detached from the system as a whole.

Conclusion

For Colombia, traditional Granger causality tests reveal little evidence of export-led growth. However, analysis of structural export change and export diversification sheds significant light on the trade-growth linkages. Our results do in fact reveal a positive interaction between structural change in the export sector and Colombian GDP growth suggesting that dynamic changes in the composition of the export sector are more significant for GDP growth than either the aggregate growth rate of exports or the degree of export diversification. We also found no significant role of exports in promoting growth through the channel of alleviating the foreign exchange constraint, as measured by growth in intermediate imports.

While there are some similarities between the Colombian experience and the case of Chile which we have previously analyzed, it remains to be seen whether the role of export diversification and export structural change can be generalized over a larger sample of developing countries. Examining these phenomena over a panel sample of developing countries remains a promising avenue for further research.

Notes

1. For earlier contributions, see Emery (1967), Kravis (1980), Krueger (1978), and Balassa (1978). The later literature, typified by tests of Granger-causality or use of cointegration methods, is represented by Jung and Marshall (1985), Bahmani-Oskooee et al. (1991), Esfahani (1991) and Serletis (1992).
2. Bahmani-Oskooee and Alse (1993), using quarterly data from 1973 to 1988 and considering log levels of the variables, fail to find significant causation in either direction between output and exports for Colombia, while finding strong bilateral causation for most of the other countries in their sample. They do, however, find the series to be co-integrated and, correspondingly, causation from output growth to export growth through the fact that the lagged error correction term is significantly different from zero. Their result is broadly consistent with ours. Yaghmaian (1994) conducts a time series analysis of 66 countries and finds export growth variable significant in 55 countries but insignificant for Colombia. Jung and Marshall (1985) find no evidence of export-led growth or growth-led exports in Colombia. Hutchison and Singh (1992), using a bivariate model, find that Colombian exports cause non-export sector domestic growth. After controlling for the rate of investment, however, the relationship between exports and growth is no longer significant.
3. An increase in REXP corresponds to a depreciation, and a decrease in REXP to an

appreciation.

4. We are indebted to an anonymous referee for this suggestion.
5. The Dickey-Fuller unit root statistic for LEXP, LGDP, and their first differences dLEXP and DLGDP were 1.11, 0.3615, 4.448 and 5.275 respectively. This indicates that LEXP and LGDP are integrated of order one. The Dickey-Fuller unit root statistic for the error terms were 1.963 and 2.122 respectively. Given that the error terms are also integrated of order one, the series are not cointegrated.
6. The sample here runs from 1967 to 1990 (n=24).
7. The sample is from 1967 to 1990 (n=24).
8. The elimination of variables for the regressions was done in the following manner. We began with a general specification that included, in their stationary form, SPECL LEXP, LGDP, DLIMP, DLREXP, DLGW, wtTRAD7, DSUBSIDY, DCOFFEE, DOIL and one period lagged values for each of the variables. To arrive at the specification reported we first minimized the Akaike information criterion over the set of possible candidate specifications in OLS. Since the set of equations obtained was under identified, we progressively reduced the number of independent variables by eliminating independent variables with little explanatory power, using the rank and order conditions for the system as a guide, until an identified system was obtained.

References

Amin Gutiérrez De Piñeres, Sheila (1996), 'Externalities in the Export Sector and Long Run Growth Rates', *Singapore Economic Review*, vol. 41, no. 1 (April), pp. 13-24.

Amin Gutiérrez De Piñeres, Sheila, and Michael J. Ferrantino (1997), 'Export Diversification and Structural Dynamics in the Growth Process: A Case Study of Chile', *Journal of Development Economics*, vol. 52, no. 2 (April), pp. 375- 391.

Bahmani-Oskooee, Mohsen and J. Alse (1993), 'Export Growth and Economic Growth: An Application of Cointegration and Error-correction Modeling', *Journal of Developing Areas,* vol. 27 (July), pp. 533-542.

Bahmani-Oskooee, M. Hamid and S. Ghiath (1991), 'Exports, Growth and Causality in LDCS: A Re-examination', *Journal of Development Economics*, vol.36, no.2, pp. 405-415.

Balassa, Bela (1978), 'Exports and Economic Growth: Further Evidence', *Journal of* Development Economics, vol. 5, no.2, pp. 181-89.

Cohen, Alvin and Frank Gunter, Eds. (1992), *The Colombian Economy: Issues of Trade and Development*, Boulder: Westview Press.

Edwards, Sebastian (1993), 'Openness, Trade Liberalization, and Growth in Developing Countries', *Journal of Economic Literature*, vol. 31, pp. 1358-1393.

Emery, Robert (1967), 'The Relation of Exports and Economic Growth', *Kyklos*, vol.20, no.4, pp.470 84.

Esfahani, Hadi (1991), 'Exports, Imports, and Economic Growth in Semi-industrialized Countries', *Journal of Development Economics*, vol. 35, no.1, pp. 93-116.

Foxley, A. (1983), *Latin American Experiments in Neo-conservative Economics*, Berkeley: University of California Press.

Hallberg, K (1991), *Colombia: Industrial Competition and Performance*. Washington, D.C.: the World Bank.

Garcia Garcia, J. and G. Montes Llamas (1988), *Coffee Boom, Government Expenditure, and Agricultural Prices: The Colombian Experience*, Research Report #68, Washington, D.C.: International Food Policy Research Institute.

Hutchison, Michael and Nirvikar Singh (1992), 'Exports, Non Exports and Externalities: A Granger Causality Approach', *International Economic Journal*, vol.6, no.2, pp. 79-94.

International Monetary Fund, *International Financial Statistics Yearbook* , various years.

Jung, Woo and Peyton Marshall (1985), 'Exports, Growth and Causality in Developing Countries', *Journal of Development Economics*, vol.18 no.2, pp. 1-12.

Kravis, Irving (1970), 'Trade as a Handmaiden of Growth', *Economic Journal*, vol. 80, no.320, pp. 850-72.

Krueger, Anne (1988), *Foreign Trade Regimes and Economic Development: Liberalization Attempts and Consequences*, Cambridge, MA: Ballinger Pub. Co. For NBER.

Ocampo, J and L. Villar (1994), 'Colombian Manufactured Exports, 1967-1991', in *Manufacturing for Export in the Developing World: Problems and Possibilities*, Edited by G.K. Helleiner, NY:Routledge.

Serletis, Apostolos (1992), 'Export Growth and Canadian Economic Development' *Journal of Development Economics*, vol. 38, no.1, pp. 133-45.

Summers, R. and A. Heston (1991), 'The Penn World Table (Mark 5): An Expanded Set of International Comparisons, 1950-1988', *Quarterly Journal of Economics*, vol. 106, no.2, pp. 327-368.

Taylor, Brian (1996), *Global Financial Data*, Alhambra, Ca.

Thoumi, Francisco (1995), *Political Economy and Illegal Drugs in Colombia*, London: Lynne Rienner Publishers.

United Nations Monthly Bulletin of Statistics, Various Years.

Yaghmaian, Behzad (1994), 'An Empirical Investigation of Exports, Development and Growth in Developing Countries: Challenging the Neoclassical Theory of Export-led Growth', in *World Development*, vol. 22, no.12, pp.1977-1995.

Worldmark Encyclopedia of the Nations (1984), Detroit, MI: Gale Research.

6 The Oil Giants: Mexico and Venezuela

Introduction

Oil is regarded by many citizens and leaders of developing countries as the panacea for their problems. This is clearly illustrated when President Lopez Portillo of Mexico declared: 'There are two kinds of countries in the world today- those that don't have oil and those that do. We have it' (Skidmore and Smith, 1992, p. 246). Mexico and Venezuela are the two largest oil-producing countries in Latin American. While other smaller countries such as Trinidad and Tobago and Ecuador are oil producers, their economies are much smaller than the two giants: Mexico and Venezuela.

Oil money is considered a rent and therefore, tends to substitute for other forms of income rather than supplement it. Oil dominated economies can experience inflation and misallocations of resources within the economy. What is interesting, however, is the role of oil dominance in these economies and export portfolios. This chapter attempts to define the export sector dynamics of these two countries and reveal how each has responded to changes in the price of oil. Also defined is the role of the political system in each country and its ability to deal with external price shocks. *De facto* single party rule in Mexico has created a more stable political climate in the face of price shocks. Venezuela, a democracy since 1958, has faced considerably more political turmoil when oil revenues have fallen.

In this chapter we examine the not only how each country's political system and democratic stability has been impacted by their lack of diversification, but also the relationship between export diversification and economic growth. Interestingly, we find there is no statistical relationship between exports and growth in Venezuela. Venezuela's dependence on oil is such that developments in the oil sector are largely autonomous with respect to the rest of the economy. Also Jorge Salazar Carrillo (1994) points out that Venezuela has failed over the years to use its oil revenues effectively for long run development projects. On the other hand, in Mexico we find that a more diversified export portfolio has had a positive impact on economic growth.

Mexico is a special case because of its close proximity to the United States and the maquiladora program along the border. Also in the case of Mexico we see that higher GDP growth is associated with a more diversified export base and higher oil prices.

The Mexican Case

In March of 1938, a historic day for Mexicans, President Lazaro Cardenas nationalized the oil industry and *Petróleos Mexicanos* (PEMEX) was born. The nationalization was a result of the failure of foreign oil companies to abide by a Mexican Supreme Court decision relating to workers' rights and was a political statement that Mexico would not be subjugated by the more developed nations. In response to the nationalization of the oil fields, the United States and Europe attempted to boycott Mexican oil. The boycott, however, was difficult to sustain due to WWII. 'Thus, although the Mexican nation was willing to endure any sacrifices to protect the dignity achieved through the expropriation of seventeen companies, these sacrifices were ameliorated by world events in the 1939-1945 period' (Velasco, p.57). PEMEX was created to manage the oil industry. PEMEX, while an oil company, had both economic and social objectives. The social objective included expanding employment and improving working conditions. As the number of employees grew, so did PEMEX's importance in the Mexican economy. PEMEX is such an important part of the Mexican economy that although the director is not officially a cabinet member, he reports directly to the President of Mexico. As PEMEX has grown, so has its power and share of government budget, making it one of the largest economic entities in Latin America.

Under Cardenas, Mexico maintained a diversified economy partially due to the secondary effects of the boycott. In the late 1970s huge oil deposits were discovered in Mexico, forever changing their export sector. The oil discovery helped fuel growth rates around 9 percent per annum. However, the GDP growth was concentrated in the cities, leading to environmental problems and urban congestion. There was a large rural-to-urban migration aggravating the existing problems in the city. Social services and infrastructure continue to be overused and underdeveloped. Living conditions of many of Mexico's poor deteriorated. 'An enduring controversy affecting PEMEX and the entire oil-related government structure has been the neglect and mistreatment of the geographical regions in which most of the oil has been produced, and most specifically the states of Chiapas and Tabasco. In Chiapas and Tabasco the oil boom has changed the face of the region profoundly, in social, economic, psychological and political dimensions' (Velasco, p.92). The initial complaints were that PEMEX was transforming the rural lifestyle at the expense of the rural population, with oil being its only concern. In this case, oil was also affecting the social character of Mexico. The wealth was used by the state to finance extravagant expenses and maintain the ruling party's position. Additionally, Mexico borrowed against its future earnings and spent lavishly without regard to the return on investments or potential interest rate increases.

In the early 1980s the price of oil plummeted, leaving many countries with large debts and no means by which to repay. Mexico, with its heavy dependence on oil revenues, was hit hard. Debt restructuring became the focus of government policy. Strict fiscal and monetary controls were instituted to stabilize the economy. Most importantly, the crisis forced Mexico to begin reducing its dependence on oil revenues. The maquiladora program was promoted, as were nontraditional exports. Table 6.1 illustrates the top five exports for Mexico in terms of real export shares, reveals how the importance of oil has declined in recent years. In 1982 oil represented 71 percent of Mexico's exports. By 1995 it was only 19 percent of total exports. The ability of Mexico to reduce its dependence of oil as a total share of exports is the first step towards building a healthier, more stable economy.

Mexico has dealt with three difficulties of an export sector dominated by one export good: an expanding surplus in the current account, rapid and unbalanced growth, and inflation. Inflation led to massive outflows of capital and the dollarization of the economy. The wealthy are usually able to anticipate the large devaluations and move their capital out while the poor and middle income groups bear the cost of the financial mismanagement of the economy by the government. The inflation contributes to worsening income inequality as the unintended effect is a transfer of wealth from the poor and middle classes to the wealthy. Additionally, the inflationary gap lowers the purchasing power of the domestic currency, encourages imports and discourages exports, decreases domestic investment, and increases capital outflows and social unrest. Capital owners are better able to survive inflation while the day laborer suffers the most.

With the oil revenues has come modernization; but modernization has many meanings. Social and cultural relationships must also change with development. This is often difficult and, if not be done gradually, can lead to domestic unrest. Until recently it was under the single-party leadership of the PRI that political stability was maintained. With modernization and new technology, access to information is now more widely dispersed among the Mexican populace. Modernization has also been supported by a more diversified export sector. This process has led to increased demands for transparency in the political process and access to the government. In Mexico, this has been manifest in the strengthening of political parties other than the PRI as well as the opening up of the PRI nominating process in a national primary for the first time in 1999.

The Venezuelan Case

Oil was discovered in Venezuela in the early 1900s, making it one of the richest countries in Latin America. Since the discovery of oil, this commodity has driven Venezuela's economy. 'By 1926, oil had displaced coffee as the country's most valuable export commodity and biggest revenue generator; by 1929, it was providing 76 percent of the country's export earnings and half the government's revenues' (Boue, p.179). Jorge Salazar-Carrillo (1994) states that the contribution of oil revenues to public revenues was on average 51.6 percent for 1958-1959, 69.5 percent for 1960-1965, 60 percent for 1965-1973. Public revenue generated from oil revenues ranged from 82 percent in 1974 to 66 percent in 1984 and 43 percent in 1986 to 82 percent again in 1990. This clearly points out the importance of oil in the Venezuelan economy. Daniel Levine points out that 'the vast impact of petroleum on Venezuelan politics and society is undeniable. The state depends utterly on oil revenues, and the economy and social structure are the way they are today as a result of changes beginning almost seventy years ago, and mediated through petroleum's impact on agriculture, industry, migration, city life, and popular culture' (Levine, p. 266). Venezuela moved from a rural agrarian society to a literate urban, service based economy with a falling median age.

Table 6.1 Top Five Real Export Shares

year	SITC	Industry Description	Venezuela			Mexico
1962	33	oil	0.975705	33	oil	0.163778
1962	67	iron and steel	0.014718	26	textile fibers	0.131953
1962	7	coffee	0.003537	68	non-ferrous metals	0.128147
1962	34	gas natural	0.002694	7	coffee	0.110333
1962	66	nonmetal mineral manufactures	9.28543E	6	sugar	0.076016
1972	33	oil	0.963213	5	fruit and vegetables	0.117567
1972	34	gas natural	0.013560	6	sugar	0.069594
1972	28	metalliferous ores	0.011169	7	coffee	0.065579
1972	6	sugar	0.002337	26	textile fibers	0.063768
1972	67	iron and steel	0.002266	68	non-ferrous metals	0.062319
1982	33	oil	0.946232	33	oil	0.717954
1982	68	non-ferrous metals	0.021861	5	fruit and vegetables	0.032186
1982	67	iron and steel	0.006772	34	natural gas	0.027080
1982	51	chemical elements	0.006632	68	non-ferrous metals	0.024011
1982	5	fruit and vegetables	0.003678	71	non-electric machinery	0.023110
1990	33	oil	0.844138	33	oil	0.440448
1990	68	non-ferrous metals	0.042364	73	transport equipment	0.106323
1990	67	iron and steel	0.025107	71	non-electric machinery	0.073697
1990	28	metalliferous ores	0.014572	5	fruit and vegetables	0.050471
1990	71	non-electric machinery	0.006382	68	non-ferrous metals	0.030919
1995	33	oil	0.793232	72	electrical machinery	0.261784
1995	60	basic manufactures	0.059126	33	oil	0.191870
1995	68	non-ferrous metals	0.026165	73	transport equipment	0.134474
1995	50	chemicals	0.021843	71	non-electric machinery	0.068057
1995	73	transport equipment	0.015246	89	misc. manufactured goods	0.035517

While some advocated using oil revenues to diversify, the government maintained a policy of using oil revenues to buy imports and subsidize basic services for its citizenry. In the 1960s social reforms were passed, financed by oil revenues. The oil industry was finally nationalized in 1976 and PdVSA was formed. The economy just continued to roll along. Oil revenues allowed Venezuela to create an urban-service oriented economy. 'Oil revenues have been recycled into the economy mostly through central state expenditures. Historically, these have focused on public works and related efforts in major cities' (Levine, p. 270). As in Mexico, Venezuelan politicians used oil revenues to placate voters, especially urban voters, with subsidies for commodities such as food and utilities. 'Subsidies were a central part of the strategy for the distribution of oil wealth. Transfers to households averaged 7 percent of the government budget over the period 1973-1978' (Boue, p.185). 'During 1960-1973, Venezuela's per capita income was just below that of the least advanced West European countries' (Boue, p.183). The Venezuelan economy grew more slowly during times of high oil prices, negating the theory that oil was the solution to their underdevelopment. Additionally, the subsidies drained Venezuela's international reserves creating a financial crisis when the price of oil fell in the early 1980s.

Salazar-Carrillo (1994) also points out that oil revenues were not used effectively for public investment and long range development projects. Oil revenues and the corresponding foreign exchange it generated allowed Venezuela to follow an import substitution strategy that was not hindered by bottlenecks that occurred in many other Latin American countries that were bound by foreign exchange constraints. Oil revenues were used by the government to finance current rather than capital expenditures. For the period 1958-1990, Salazar-Carrillo finds that oil revenues were not utilized efficiently or effectively to guarantee Venezuela's economic development. In most cases increased revenue was used to finance public expenditures or alleviate import constraints to sustain the import substitution policy that produced manufactured goods for the domestic economy. However, unlike Mexico, Venezuela did not have a strong central governing party, making her more susceptible to social unrest during times of economic crisis. When the oil crisis hit, Venezuela was unable to meet its debt obligations. The debt crisis led to a massive devaluation and removal of certain public subsidies. Levine points out that the crisis of the 1980s was a result of 'the collapse of world oil demand and prices. The sudden drop in prices for Venezuela's key product brought devaluation, economic stagnation, and a major spurt in unemployment' (p. 282). The result was political and social unrest. 'Venezuela erupted in a series of nationwide riots and looting from 27 February to 3 March, 1989, which left scores of people dead and thousands injured' (Boue, p.188).

Venezuela's attempts at economic diversification have been largely unsuccessful. 'In 1991, PdVSA was still responsible for 24 percent of the country's GNP, 86 percent of its foreign exchange earnings and 83 percent of the government's tax revenue' (Boue, p.188). Oil continues to be the key export and maintain the largest share in the export portfolio. Even today Venezuela's economy is closely tied to oil prices. Table 6.1 reveals that from the early 1960s through the 1980s oil represented at least 95 percent of Venezuela's real exports. Even in 1995, oil still maintains a 75 percent share of real exports, by far dominating the export sector.

Using a variety of indices, we analyze the export sectors of Mexico and Venezuela. Mexico has been able to reduce the dominance of oil, largely because of its relationship with the United States; while, Venezuela has been unable to diversify its export portfolio. U.S. influence in Venezuela has mainly been limited to its predominance as an oil exporter. The U.S. supported the military regimes prior to 1958 because of a belief that a strong central military rule would guarantee stable oil exports. Support for multi-party democracy came only with the threat of Castro in Cuba. U.S. investment in Venezuela was limited to the petroleum sector.

On the other hand, U.S. influence in Mexico goes beyond its reliance on oil exports. Mexico is the United State's neighbor and major export market justifying a more direct role. NAFTA is a clear example of this. Additionally, 'foreign direct investment (FDI) has played a decisive role in Mexican economic development. Different sectors have been the main recipients of FDI at different times. Right after the colonial period, England became the largest foreign investor in Mexico, a role assumed by the United States since the early decades of this century' (Nicholson, et al, p.1). In the early years, foreign investment in Mexico was in mining and transportation; however, in the postwar era, investment has been largely directed towards the manufacturing sector. This, coupled with dependence on foreign exchange from commerce and tourism with the United States has left the Mexican government with little choice but to accept guidance of its economic policy from the United States. Smith and Skidmore state that, 'however much Mexicans wanted to achieve economic sovereignty, in fact they retained intimate ties to their northern neighbor' (p. 245). While oil allowed Mexico to reduce some of their dependence on the United States in terms of commerce and tourism, economic integration with the United States has continued a pace. The bailout after the peso crisis in 1994 illustrated the commitment of the United States to maintaining stability in Mexico.

Data and Analysis

Basic Data

Two-digit SITC export data from the United Nations trade database for the years 1962-1993 were used to derive empirical measures of the 'traditionality' of specific export industries, described below, as well as measures of the degree of export diversification and structural change taking place in Colombia's export portfolio. Nominal export values were deflated by appropriate product specific price deflators. Primary commodities were deflated using commodity price indices from the United Nations *Monthly Bulletin of Statistics* and IMF *International Financial Statistics*. Manufactures were deflated by their appropriate U.S. producer price index, using the general U.S. producer price index when an industry-level one was not available. In the regression analysis we use the following variables: the growth rate of real GDP (GC), from the International Comparisons Project (Summers and Heston, 1991); world growth rates (GW), derived from IMF-IFS data; real exports (GEXP), as aggregated from our deflated two-digit SITC data. We calculate the value of imported intermediate inputs (IMP) in much the same way as in Esfahani (1991). The variable IMP is composed of the value of imports of crude materials, mineral fuels, animal/vegetable oil and fats, chemicals less pharmaceuticals and perfumes/cosmetics, basic manufactures, and machinery/transport equipment less road vehicles and planes. The price of oil (DPOIL) is the U.N. commodity price index for oil.

Measures of Export Specialization and Structural Change

Calculating the Traditionality Index (TRAD7) A relatively constant aggregate level of diversification may mask a substantial degree of structural transformation in a country's comparative advantage, if different product groups are replacing each other in rapid succession. To address this we use a medium run measure of structural change, TRAD7, to identify dynamics in the export sector (see chapter Two for details as to the construction of the index). The first measure, TRAD7, is the variance of traditionality scores using seven-year intervals rather than the full sample period. Thus, we have values of TRAD7 for 1965-1990; the value for 1965, e.g. is the variance of the 52

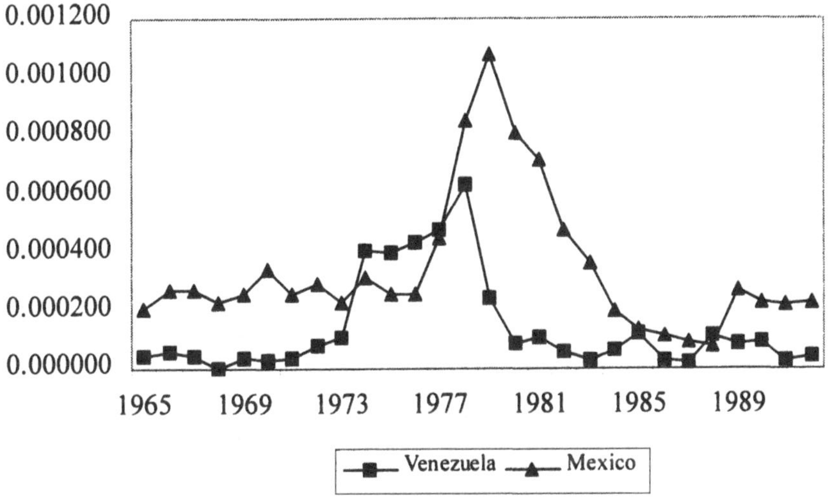

Figure 6.1 Weighted TRAD7

industry values of T_i obtained using the period 1962-1968 as a reference period. When the variance is high, this implies that the industries experienced relatively divergent patterns of export growth during the period, with some being leaders and some laggers, so that a high variance is interpreted as an episode of structural change centered on the period in question. A low variance implies that the composition of exports was relatively stable over the 7-year period. Given that Mexico and Venezuela have one export, oil, that dominates its export portfolio we also constructed a weighted TRAD7 index (WTRAD7). WTRAD7 weighs each traditionality score by the real export share of that industry for that specific year, then calculates the variance. This allows us to capture the influence of the predominant export sectors, such as oil and coffee, on the TRAD7 index.[1] The weighted index is used in the subsequent regression analysis. Visually, a high value of WTRAD7 corresponds to a large dispersion among curves of the type shown in Figure 6.1, and vice versa.

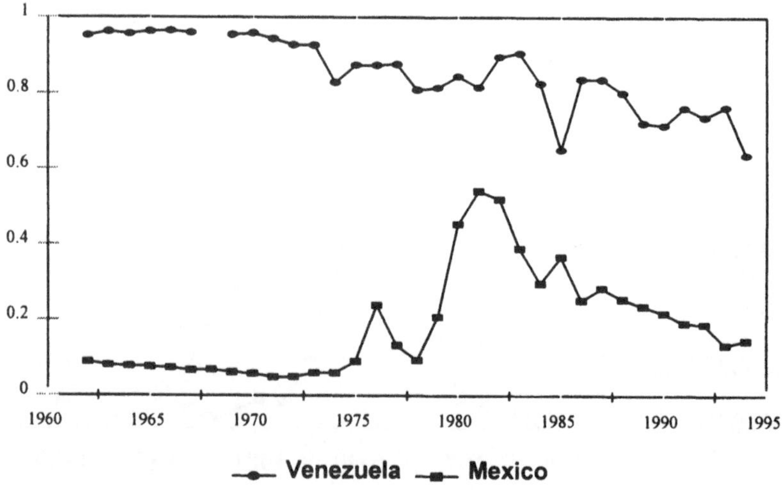

Figure 6.2 Specialization Index

What is interesting about the weighted TRAD7 is that while the specialization measure reveals that oil has dominated Venezuela's export sector, there has been considerable medium run structural change (See Figure 6.1). A changing portfolio of secondary exports, excluding oil, could explain this. In Mexico we see more medium run change, especially during the late 1970s and early 1980s. In the late 1970s, there is an increase in structural change as Mexico expands its export of manufactures and transport equipment, as the maquiladora program expands.

Tables 6.2 and 6.3 show the dynamic changes in each country's export portfolios. The tables list the nontraditional exports first with the last export listed being the most traditional export. (See Chapter Four on the comparison of sectors by traditionality.) The last column represents the total cumulative dollar value of exports in real terms over the entire period studied. The interesting result is that for Mexico the nontraditional exports represent a significant share of total exports while for Venezuela the nontraditional exports are a much smaller share. This indicates that Mexico's nontraditional export sector is more dynamic and growing.

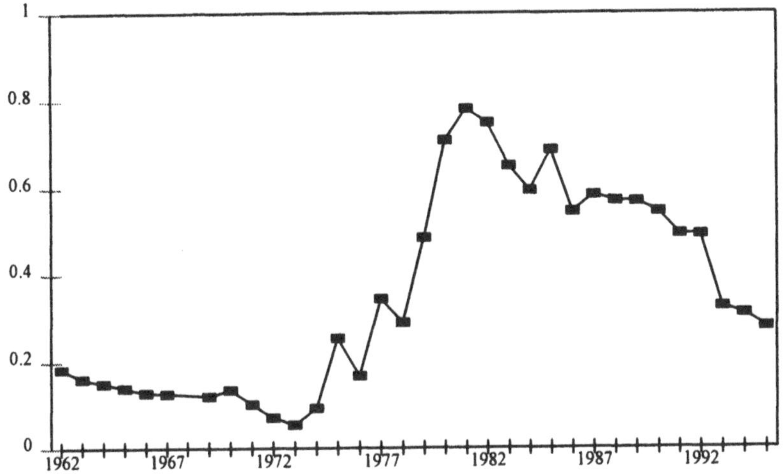

Figure 6.3 Export Similarity Index- Mexico/Venezuela

Calculating the Specialization Index (SPECL) The SPECL index constructed for these countries also reflects the concentration of exports by Venezuela in oil and the diversification of the Mexican export sector (see Chapter Two for details as to the construction of index), see Figure 6.2. SPECL thus takes on values approaching 1 if the country's exports are concentrated in a single commodity classification and values approaching 0 as exports become diversified. Venezuela's SPECL index is concentrated around 1 indicating a highly specialized export portfolio. On the other hand, Mexico's SPECL remains below .4 except during the oil shock and debt crisis years; and moves to below .2 in the early 1990s. Mexico's export portfolio only reveal signs of specialization during the oil dominated years of the late 1970s and early 1980s. While Venezuela has failed to diversify, Mexico did diversify in response to falling oil prices. Chapter Three discusses how Venezuela's diversification experience compares against all other Latin American countries. Venezuela remains the most specialized economy in Latin America, and, thus, more susceptible to a single commodity price shock.

Calculating the Export Similarity Index (ESI) In constructing the ESI, we utilized two-digit SITC export data from the United Nations trade database for the years 1962-1995 for Mexico and Venezuela. The ESI varies between 0 and 1 with 1 indicating that two countries share an identical export commodity portfolio and 0 indicating a completely dissimilar portfolio (see Chapter Three for methodology). Figure 6.3 illustrates the ESI for the country pair of Mexico and Venezuela. The year 1968 should be excluded because there is no data for Venezuela. The years in which the countries are most similar are post oil shock years and debt crisis years as they both relied on their oil exports for foreign exchange. During these years the ESI averaged in the .65 range; however, by 1994 and 1995 their export portfolios showed significant signs of divergence as the ESI is around .3. Looking at the real value of export shares also reveals how Venezuela has continued to rely on oil while Mexico has begun to diversify (for more on the relationship of these countries' export portfolios with those of other Latin American countries see Chapter Three).

Additionally, we calculated the top five exports for both countries in real terms as a share of total exports. Since the dollar value of oil exports is significant using shares allows us to capture the dynamics occurring in each country's export portfolio. The results by ten-year intervals are presented in Table 6.1. From 1962 to 1995, oil dominates Venezuela's exports. It ranges from 97 percent of exports in 1962 to 79 percent in 1995. All other exports in the top five have less than 5 percent of the share of total exports. Mexico's export portfolio is significantly more dynamic. The only period for which oil dominates exports is in the early 1980s; in 1982, oil represented 71 percent of exports. Oil was the top export in 1962, but combined with the other top four export only represented 52 percent of Mexico's exports. In 1972 oil does not even make the top five. In 1990 oil remains at the top but there is an emergence of other exports such as transport equipment and machinery revealing the growing maquiladora program. By 1995, oil moves to second place and only represents 19 percent of total exports. The top export is electrical machinery. All other exports in the top five are transport equipment, electrical machinery, machinery, and miscellaneous manufactures, all reflective of a thriving maquiladora program. The Mexican economy has reduced its reliance on oil, allowing it to better respond to external shocks.

Table 6.2 Causality Tests (standard errors in parentheses)

MEXICO

	Dependent variable			
Independent variables	1a DLGDP	2a DLEXP	3a DLGDP	4a DLEXP
INTERCEPT	.01076**	.02117	.007116*	.01276
	(.004761)	(.02456)	(.0031759)	(.02562)
DLGDP1	.4826**	1.5867	.6637***	2.3482**
	(.1865)	(.9631)	(.1655)	(1.1282)
DLEXP1	-.0271	-.3020	-.0482	-.3208
	(.03762)	(.1942)	(.02912)	(.1984)
DLIMP			.06577**	.01747
			(.01864)	(.1270)
DLIMP1			-.04629**	-.1944
			(.02170)	(.1479)
N	24	24	24	24
R^2	.2386	.174	.5985	.2412

VENEZUELA

	Dependent variable			
Independent variables	1b DLGDP	2b DLEXP	3b DLGDP	4b DLEXP
INTERCEPT	.008356	-.002061	.007049	-.005342
	(.004842)	(.02647)	(.005151)	(.02833)
DLGDP1	.1308	-1.3430	.3441	-.5771
	(.2236)	(1.2226)	(.3102)	(1.7064)
DLEXP1	-.0112	-.2631	-.01729	-.3220
	(.0388)	(.2125)	(.04181)	(.2299)
DLIMP			-.04770	-.1967
			(.04712)	(.2591)
DLIMP1			-.000185	-.1252
			(.03754)	(.2064)
N	21	21	21	21
R^2	.022	.125	.0786	.1658

* - significant at .10 ** - significant at .05 *** - significant at .01

Relationship between Exports and Output In the following discussion, the letter 'D' preceding a variable name denotes its first-differenced value throughout, while the number '1' following a variable name denotes its one-year lagged value. The time series LEXP (natural log real exports) and LGDP (natural log real GDP) are I(1); that is, they are stationary in first differences. Thus, it is appropriate to perform standard Granger-Sims causality tests on the first differences of the two variables, i.e. on their growth rates (cf. Serletis, 1992):[2]

DLEXP = f(DLEXP1, DLGDP1) (1)
DLGDP = g(DLEXP1, DLGDP1) (2)

The results are reported in Table 6.2. We do not find strong evidence for export-led growth in the Granger sense for Mexico or Venezuela. In the case of Mexico we find that last period's GDP has a positive influence on this period's GDP. Yet, the question remains in what manner exports could affect growth. Another possible channel through which exports may affect domestic growth is by reducing foreign exchange constraints. Easing of the constraint should facilitate the purchase of intermediate inputs and relieve bottlenecks in the production process (Esfahani, 1991). We expanded equations 1 and 2 to include current and lagged values of the natural log of the imported intermediate inputs (LIMP). The general regression model is as follows and the results are reported in Table 6.2:

DLEXP = f(DLEXP1, DLGDP1, DLIMP, DLIMP1) (3)
DLGDP = g(DLEXP1, DLGDP1, DLIMP, DLIMP1) (4)

All variables remain insignificant for Venezuela; however, for Mexico there appears to be a more dynamic relationship in place. In the case of Mexico, we find a positive relationship between growth and previous period growth and current period imports of intermediate inputs. This could be a result of Mexico's strong maquiladora program or of a foreign exchange constraint. There is no obvious motivation for the negative relationship between growth and previous period imports of intermediate inputs. We also find that for Mexico that there is a positive relationship between previous period growth and exports. However, this result does not indicate the manner in which the export sector affects the growth rate of an economy. We propose to answer that question by studying the impact of the structural change and diversification in the export sector and its impact on domestic and export growth rates.

Relationship Among Export Structural Change, Exports, and Output In order to move beyond simple tests of Granger causality we attempted to include our variables that characterize the dynamics of the export sector in the models that explain export and GDP growth rates.[3] The system of equations estimated for each country are as follows:[4]

Mexico

DLGDP=F(DSPECL1, DLEXP, DLGDP1, DLIMP, DGW, DPOIL) (5a)
DLEXP= G(DSPECL, DLEXP1, DLGDP1, DGW, DPOIL) (6a)
DWTRAD7= H(DLEXP1, DLGDP, DGW1, DWTTRAD71) (7a)
DSPECL= J(DLEXP, DLIMP, DGW, DWTTRAD71, DPOIL) (8a)
DLIMP=K(DSPECL1, DLGDP, DLGP1, DWTTRAD71) (9a)

Venezuela

DLGDP=F(DSPECL, DLIMP, DGW, DPOIL) (5b)
DLEXP= G(DSPECL, DWTTRAD7, DPOIL) (6b)
DWTRAD7= H(DSPECL, DLEXP1, DLGDP, DWTTRAD71) (7b)
DSPECL= J(DLEXP, DWTTRAD7, DPOIL, DPOIL1) (8b)
DLIMP=K(DLGDP1, DGW1, DPOIL) (9b)

The results are reported in Table 6.3. Each individual equation was estimated by OLS, and the system was estimated using three-stage least squares (3SLS). The system is reported as equations 10(a)-14(a) for Mexico and 10(b)- 14(b) for Venezuela in Table 6.3. The principal features of the system are robust to the manner in which simultaneity is handled.

The GDP growth equation (eq. 5 and 10) indicates that Mexican growth is positively related to the price of oil and last period's growth. Additionally, a more diversified export portfolio has a positive effect on economic growth in Mexico, although the strength and statistical significance of this effect is stronger in OLS than when the system is estimated as a whole. Higher world growth rates are related to more exports, more structural change, and more diversification in Mexico. This implies a growing and healthy Mexican economy is tied to a booming world economy, more than likely reflecting the close ties between the U.S. and Mexican economies. The effect of diversification and world growth on Mexican GDP is strong in OLS but weaker in the system.

Table 6.3 Structural Regressions (standard errors in parentheses)

Mexico

	OLS Dependent variables				
Independent variables	5a DLGDP	6a DLEXP	7a DWTRAD7	8a DSPECL	9a DLIMP
INTERCEPT	.001369	.03382*	-.000001018	-.03413***	-.02121
	(.003357)	(.02011)	(.00004860)	(.01183)	(.03561)
DSPECL		.5563***			
		(.1552)			
DSPECL1	-.0807***				.5762*
	(.02806)				(.2837)
DLEXP	-.01672			.6832***	
	(.02599)			(.1367)	
DLEXP1		-.2988**	-.000477		
		(.1462)	(.000381)		
DWTRAD7					
DWTRAD71			.2294	209.471***	-321.516**
			(.2222)	(80.8284)	(144.9986)
DPOIL	.02927***	-.0436		-.0444	
	(.0089)	(.05316)		(.05359)	
DPOIL1					
DLGDP			.001278		6.9317***
			(.00196)		(1.3576)
DLGDP1	.8162***	.9255			-3.8965**
	(.1639)	(.8791)			(1.6469)
DGW	.1373	2.084***		-1.2743**	
	(.1295)	(.7447)		(.6723)	
DGW1			.003343*		
			(.001679)		
DLIMP	.05974***			.3083***	
	(.01565)			(.0907)	
DLIMP1					
N	24	24	24	24	24
R^2	.778	.6135	.3058	.716	.5986

* - significant at .10 ** - significant at .05 *** - significant at .01

Table 6.3 Continued

Mexico

	3SLS Dependent variables				
Independent variables	10a DLGDP	11a DLEXP	12a DWTRAD7	13a DSPECL	14a DLIMP
INTERCEPT	.003553 (.005698)	.0275 (.02998)	-.00001977 (.00005898)	-.0405* (.0209)	-.01425 (.03327)
DSPECL		.3609 (.5029)			
DSPECL1	-.05963 (.05479)				.4529 (.2657)
DLEXP	-.02308 (.07309)			.4149 (.2672)	
DLEXP1		-.3168* (.1716)	-.000494 (.000363)		
DWTRAD7					
DWTRAD71				391.0829** (155.3656)	-325.788** (144.335)
DPOIL	.03794** (.01752)	-.02597 (.0610)	.1539 (.2321)	-.1565 (.1008)	
DPOIL1					
DLGDP			.002241 (.002644)		5.8375*** (1.9935)
DLGDP1	.7934*** (.2932)	1.314 (1.5744)			-3.1537* (1.6572)
DGW	.1853 (.21088)	2.155*** (.799)		-1.03735 (.7817)	
DGW1		.002786* (.001550)			
DLIMP	.01304 (.07312)			.8314* (.4180)	
DLIMP1					
N	System Weighted MSE 2.6498 with 96 degrees of freedom				
R^2	System Weighted R^2 .3262				

* - significant at .10 ** - significant at .05 *** - significant at .01

Table 6.3 Continued

Venezuela

	OLS Dependent variables				
Independent variables	5b DLGDP	6b DLEXP	7b DWTRAD7	8b DSPECL	9b DLIMP
INTERCEPT	.01092**	-.01237	-.00002257	-.009069	-.03637
	(.004382)	(.01623)	(.0002060)	(.01059)	(.02277)
DSPECL	.06875	-.6419**	-.001044***		
	(.06356)	(.2713)	(.0002634)		
DSPECL1					
DLEXP				-.3536**	
				(.1363)	
DLEXP1			.000792***		
			(.0001982)		
DWTRAD7		-536.0852***		-317.0317**	
		(150.7475)		(111.6667)	
DWTRAD71			.3971**		
			(.1828)		
DPOIL		-.2562***		-.02076***	-.05455
		(.0801)		(.06361)	(.09066)
DPOIL1	.009197			-.074046	
	(.0208)			(.05108)	
DLGDP			.001991*		
			(.0009832)		
DLGDP1					4.9765***
					(1.0379)
DGW	.3032				
	(.2771)				
DGW1					-2.7099**
					(1.2690)
DLIMP	-.009517				
	(.03348)				
DLIMP1				.2080*	
				(.09881)	
N	21	21	21	21	21
R^2	.1307	.6132	.6436	.645	.5853

* - significant at .10 ** - significant at .05 *** - significant at .01

Table 6.3 Continued

Venezuela

	3SLS Dependent variables				
Independent variables	10b DLGDP	11b DLEXP	12b DWTRAD7	13b DSPECL	14b DLIMP
INTERCEPT	.008446*	-.01423	-.00002924	-.01228	-.03038
	(.004810)	(.01663)	(.00002861)	(.01086)	(.02178)
DSPECL	-.03855	-.8019**	-.001127***		
	(.08426)	(.3676)	(.000327)		
DSPECL1					
DLEXP				-.6885***	
				(.1989)	
DLEXP1			.000814***		
			(.00179)		
DWTRAD7		-703.5546***		-541.4145***	
		(195.1099)		(157.1473)	
DWTRAD71			.3948**		
			(.1747)		
DPOIL		-.2442***		-.2454***	-.1019
		(.08420)		(.07126)	(.07374)
DPOIL1	.00947			-.0454	
	(.01920)			(.04481)	
DLGDP			.002608		
			.002177)		
DLGDP1					4.5991***
					(.8658)
DGW	.4969**				
	(.2345)				
DGW1					-2.3316**
					(1.0626)
DLIMP	.08268**				
	(.03876)				
DLIMP1				.1283	
				(.08691)	
N	System Weighted MSE 1.6206 with 86 degrees of freedom				
R^2	System Weighted R^2 .556				

* - significant at .10 ** - significant at .05 *** - significant at .01

In Venezuela, however, we find that the price of oil is a more important factor. Both oil price increases and increased export specialization are associated with slower real export growth, and specialization is also associated with slower structural change. So in Venezuela a more diversified export portfolio and more rapid structural change lead to higher real exports. While a more dynamic export sector has a positive impact on overall exports the results show no link between exports and economic growth.

Conclusion

While some policy makers of developing countries believe that oil is the solution to their problem of development, more often oil revenues have been used to mask the basic problems of a developing country. Most countries with large oil revenues have used that income to placate voters and finance large budget deficits that leave the country in economic, and often political, crisis when the price of oil falls. Mexico, a more diversified economy, has fared better than that of the oil dominated economy of Venezuela. Dependence of oil to remedy the problems has left Venezuela vulnerable to single commodity price shocks and the political instability associated with external shocks to the economy. Mexico, with the help of the its largest neighboring trade partner, the United States, has diversified its economy and increased its capacity to withstand the ramifications of falling oil prices. The presence of *de facto* single party rule may have made these changes easier to implement. Today we see that Mexico is able to maintain political stability and transition into a multi-party democracy while Venezuela is facing political turmoil, as oil prices continue to fall. Therefore, while oil revenues can be used to ease the transition from a developing to a newly industrializing country, it is useful for countries to diversify their export base.

Notes

1. We are indebted to an anonymous referee for this suggestion.
2. The sample here runs from 1968 to 1992 for Mexico and 1971-1992 for Venezuela.
3. The sample here runs from 1968 to 1992 for Mexico and 1971-1992 for Venezuela.
4. The elimination of variables for the regressions was done in the following manner. We began with a general specification that included, in their stationary form, DSPECL, DLEXP, DLGDP, DLIMP, DLREXP, DGW, DWTTRAD7, DPOIL and one period lagged values for each of the variables. To arrive at the specification reported we first minimized the Akaike information criterion over the set of possible candidate specifications in OLS. Since the set of equations obtained was under identified, we progressively reduced the

number of independent variables by eliminating independent variables with little explanatory power, using the rank and order conditions for the system as a guide, until an identified system was obtained.

References

Allen, Loring (1993), *Venezuelan Economic Development; A Politico-Economic Analysis,* Greenwich, Connecticut: JAI Press.

Boue, Juan Carlos (1993) *Venezuela: the Political Economy of Oil,* Oxford: Oxford University Press.

Carrada-Bravo, Francisco (1982), *Oil, Money, and the Mexican Economy; A Macroeconomic Analysis,* Boulder, Colorado: Westview Press.

El Maliaakah, Ragaei, Oystein Noreng, and Barry W, Poulson, (1984), *Petroleum and Economic Development.* Lexington, Massachusetts: Lexington Books.

Levine, Daniel (1989), 'Venezuela: The Nature, Sources and Prospects of Democracy', in *Democracy in Developing Countries: Latin America* edited by Larry Diamond, Juan J. Linz, and Seymour Martin Lipset, Boulder, Co: Lynne Rienner Publishers.

Lieuwen, Edwin (1954), *Petroleum in Venezuela; A History,.* New York: Russell & Russell.

Nicholson, Joel, Juan España and Sheila Amin Gutiérrez de Piñeres (1998), 'Government Regulations and FDI: A historical perspective of Mexico', working paper.

Randall, Laura (1987), *The Political Economy of Venezuelan Oil,* New York: Praeger Publishers.

Salazar-Carrillo (1994), *Oil and Development in Venezuela During the Twentieth Century,* Westport, CT: Praeger Publishers.

Skidmore, Thomas and Peter H. Smith, (1992), *Modern Latin America*, 3rd edition., New York: Oxford University Press.

Teichman, Judith (1988), *Policymaking in Mexico,* Boston: Allen & Unwin.

Velasco-S, Jesus-Augustin, (1983), *Impacts of Mexican Oil Policy on Economic and Political Development,* Lexington, Massachusetts: Lexington Books.

7 Export Sector Dynamics and Growth: An international comparison

Introduction

Is there any systematic relationship between export diversification and economic growth in Latin America? If diversification is good for growth, are there any particular policies which encourage it? It is widely believed that excessive specialization in individual primary products, such as coffee, tin, copper, fruit, and petroleum, has harmed Latin American economic growth. Countries dependent on a single primary export are exposed to greater price risk and (for non-extractive exports) agro-climatic risk than are countries with a diversified export portfolio, which may lead to an unstable supply of foreign exchange and constrain investment. Furthermore, if the worldwide distribution of technical advances fluctuates unpredictably from industry to industry over time, it may be that countries which can successfully produce (and export) a wider range of goods are better equipped to exploit a larger share of the expanding technology pool, and may also have more extensive forward and backward linkages to technologically progressive sectors. For all these reasons, some form of export diversification may potentially be helpful to growth. More controversial, but long taken seriously in Latin America, was the Prebisch/Singer hypothesis that the terms of trade turn secularly against primary product exports. All of these arguments may be advanced in support of the notion that export diversification may potentially be beneficial to economic growth. Nonetheless, systematic attempts to assess this hypothesis are difficult to identify. The present effort hopefully provides some modest excuse for submitting economists to yet another 'mindless cross-country regression' in the neoclassical tradition.

In previous work (Amin Gutiérrez de Piñeres and Ferrantino, 1997a) we showed that since at least the early 1960s, there has been a long-run trend toward export diversification in Latin America which has persisted through both inward- and outward-looking policy experiments, and over a variety of macroeconomic conditions. This export diversification has typically consisted more in a diversification among primary-product exports than in an increase in manufacturing exports. According to our measure of medium-run structural change, TRAD7 (see chapters Three and Four), which captures the rate at which 'non-traditional' exports replace 'traditional' exports, showed that for most countries, structural change in exports accelerated during the late 1970s, slowed down during the debt crisis years, and reaccelerated during the 1990s. These stylized facts suggest no particular association between economic growth and export diversification. Time-series analysis of individual country growth patterns on annual data yield insights but no broad generalizations. For Chile, decreases in export specialization and acceleration in export structural change are associated with slower export growth, and export specialization is also associated with higher GDP growth. (Amin Gutiérrez de Piñeres and Ferrantino, 1997b). For Colombia, by contrast, accelerated structural change in exports is associated with more rapid GDP growth, and there is no particular relationship between the level of export specialization and GDP growth (Amin Gutiérrez de Piñeres and Ferrantino, 1999).

In this chapter, we examine the specialization/structural change/growth relationship using a larger sample of eighteen Latin American countries, and updating our measures of diversification and structural change through 1995. The empirical framework is of the standard type used for examining the properties of the neoclassical growth model, using an appropriate panel data estimator which allows for country-specific differences in labor productivity (Islam, 1995). We are mindful of the fact that estimation over a sample of Latin American countries alone implies a more restricted sample than is commonly used in the cross-country growth regression. To take account of this, we estimate a model without diversification/structural change effects, and test for differences between Latin America, sub-Saharan Africa and developing Asia in rates of convergence and long-run determinants of productivity. This in effect permits the parameters of both the aggregate production function and the sub-function determining levels of labor productivity to be region-specific, a result for which there is some empirical support. For example, Chua (1993) found that inclusion of a distance-based spillover effect for investment in the neoclassical growth equation accounted for some 14-18 percent of country-specific economic growth and helped explain away much of the effect of dummy variables for Latin America and Africa.

We find that for Latin America as a whole over the last 35 years, episodes of export diversification have indeed been associated with more rapid economic growth. This effect is economically sizable but poorly determined statistically in OLS, but becomes larger and statistically significant using a fixed-effects estimator. These estimates imply that a relatively diversified exporter such as Argentina enjoys an advantage of 0.6 percent (OLS) to nearly 3 percent (fixed effects) per year in per capita income growth relative to a relatively specialized exporter such as Venezuela. A negative relationship between export structural change and economic growth is found in both samples, but does not pass statistical significance, nor, in our preferred specification, does it achieve economic importance. This result, combined with the results of our earlier time-series analysis, suggests that the mechanisms by which structural change in the pattern of exports accelerates or decelerates are likely to be country- and situation-specific and bear no regular relationship to the business cycle.

We also find evidence for significant differences between regional production functions. Intra-regional convergence of income is stronger in Latin America than in either sub-Saharan Africa or developing Asia. The productivity effects of investment are highest in Latin America and lowest in sub-Saharan Africa. The additional productivity boost derived from foreign direct investment is also higher in Latin America than in sub-Saharan Africa. The effects of open economic policies on economic growth, using the measure of Sachs and Warner (1995), are easier to detect in the sample including all three regions. Comparisons between developing Asia and the other two regions are sensitive to the inclusion or exclusion of country-specific productivity effects.

Patterns of Diversification and Growth in Latin America

As in earlier work, we define an index of export specialization for country I in time t as

$$SPECL_{i,t} = \sum_{j=1}^{N} (s_{j,t})^2$$

where j ∈ (1,N) indexes export sectors at the two-digit SITC level. The variable for export specialization operates essentially like a Herfindahl-Hirschman index, taking values which approach 1 for a completely specialized exporter and which approach 0 otherwise.

Figure 7.1 graphs the export specialization index for the nineteen countries in our sample, taken as a simple average over 1962-1994. As can be seen, export diversification for the typical Latin American country has increased steadily over time, from about 0.42 in the early 1960s (corresponding to two or three equal-sized 2-digit SITC export industries, with nothing else) to about 0.2 in the mid-1990s (corresponding to about five equal-sized export industries). While relatively little diversification took place from about 1975-1990, the trend toward diversification may have accelerated in the 1990s. Otherwise, diversification appears to persist over periods of import substitution and trade liberalization, of expansion and recession, of debt crisis and open capital markets.

Table 7.1 looks at export specialization and growth for the nineteen countries in our sample individually, showing average export specialization over 1961-1965 and 1991-1995; annualized per capita income growth over the 35-year period from 1960-1995 and over the more recent 10-year period of 1985-1995.

While there is some coincidence between increasing diversification and strong or improving growth performance, there are exceptions to the rule as well. Chile, Colombia, Uruguay, Costa Rica, El Salvador, Paraguay and Bolivia have experienced significant diversification and relatively strong growth performance. Venezuela, Trinidad and Tobago, and Ecuador, all oil exporters, have remained relatively specialized and experienced weaker growth. Other slow-growth or negative-growth economies began relatively diversified in the early 1960s but did not diversify much further, or moved in the direction of specialization (Mexico, Peru, Nicaragua). Jamaica and Panama are examples of countries which have bucked the trend; Jamaica showing strong growth performance while specializing and Panama combining deteriorating growth with diversification. Jamaica and Panama are also unusual in their commodity pattern of exports, showing sharp swings in their patterns of specialization which are dissimilar to other countries in the region (Amin Gutiérrez de Piñeres and Ferrantino, forthcoming).

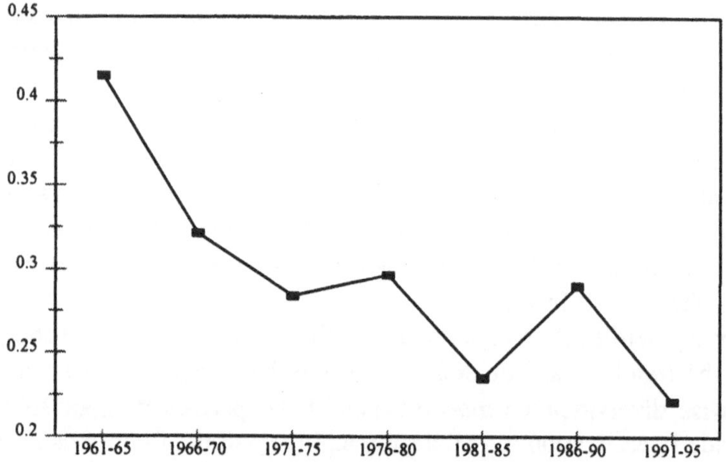

Figure 7.1 SPECL Index- Simple Average

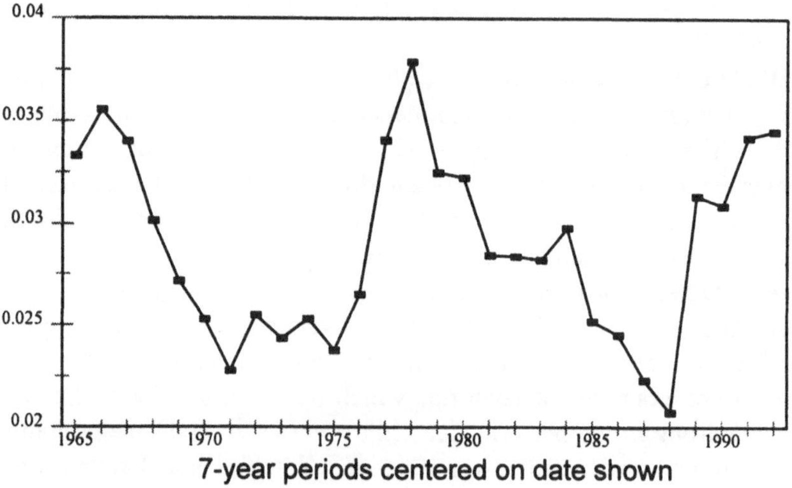

Figure 7.2 Export Structural Change

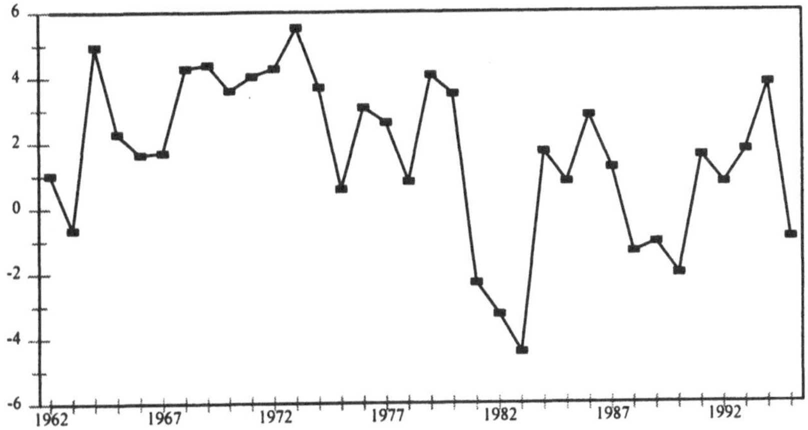

Figure 7.3 Per Capita Income Growth

We also generate a measure of export structural change over seven-year periods (see Chapter Two). This measure we have referred to earlier as TRAD7. That is, export structural change for 1975 is calculated using the seven years of data from 1972-1978, and so on. It should be noted that while some degree of export structural change is necessary for export diversification to take place, the two are not always identical; for example, there can be a good deal of medium-run churning in export structure without substantial diversification taking place.

Figure 7.2 illustrates the average performance of our measure of export structural change over time for the 19 countries in our sample, while Figure 7.3 shows per capita income growth for the Latin America/ Caribbean region as a whole, drawn from World Bank data. Structural transformation in a typical country's exports exhibits three peaks; in 1965-1967, 1977-1978, and 1991-1992 (note that because of the necessity of observing several years of data on either side of the year in question, the series on structural change is truncated at both ends, and these include our peaks). Each of these periods showed relatively strong economic growth. The troughs in structural change

Table 7.1 Export Diversification and Growth

Country	Export specialization index	Export specialization index	Annual per capita income growth	Annual per capita income growth
	1961-65	1991-95	1960-95	1985-95
Chile	0.568	0.152	0.84	4.26
Jamaica	0.221	0.291	0.87	2.78
Colombia	0.427	0.151	1.76	2.00
Uruguay	0.259	0.080	0.24	1.98
Costa Rica	0.361	0.145	1.48	1.72
El Salvador	0.490	0.236	0.64	1.19
Paraguay	0.165	0.379	1.84	1.16
Bolivia	0.593	0.190	0.45	1.12
Guatemala	0.381	0.170	0.91	0.65
Argentina	0.148	0.021	0.30	0.19
Brazil	0.401	0.058	2.22	0.05
Ecuador*	0.456	0.349	2.08	0.03
Honduras	0.359	0.279	0.81	-0.06
Panama	0.721	0.034	2.25	-0.45
Mexico	0.081	0.181	1.96	-0.51
Venezuela	0.959	0.725	-0.37	-0.72
Trinidad and Tobago	0.913	0.401	0.52	-1.19
Peru	0.158	0.139	-0.61	-2.19
Nicaragua	0.225	0.165	-1.34	-3.00

Source for columns 1 and 2: Authors' calculations. For columns 3 and 4: World Bank
*Growth reported in column 3 is for 1965-96.

occurred in 1970-1975, at about the time of the first oil crisis, and 1985-1988, during the period of retrenchment from the debt crisis. The debt crisis episode itself featured a marked deceleration of the rate of export structural change, from an average value of .0379 in 1978 to .0207 in 1988. At first glance, this pattern is suggestive of Schumpeterian structural change taking place during good times, while periods of external shock and internal adjustment require a retrenchment and refocus on the principal primary commodity.

In short, perusal of the raw data suggests an apparent lack of any relationship between export specialization/diversification and economic growth, while export structural change appears to be positively related to economic growth. As we shall see, neither one of these conclusions persists when other likely determinants of growth are controlled for.

Empirical Specification

The theoretical foundations behind the empirical exploration of the causes of economic growth in cross-country regression are by now familiar; a widely accessible exposition is Barro and Sala-I-Martin, 1995, particularly chapters Five and Twelve. A generalized expression for the rate of per capita income growth takes the form

$$Dy_t = F(y_{t-1}, h_{t-1} \mid A)$$

in which $Dy_t \equiv dy_t/y_t$ represents the growth rate of per capita income measured over a suitably long period, y_{t-1} is the initial level of per capita income, h_t is the initial level of human capital, and A is a vector of control variables. A negative relationship between initial per capita income and the growth rate of per capita income arises in the Solow-Swan model of neoclassical growth when income is below its long-run equilibrium value; lower incomes imply low capital-labor ratios, which imply a higher marginal product of capital, and thus higher returns to a given rate of savings.

A more negative coefficient on y_t (higher in absolute value) implies a more rapid rate of convergence between low- and high-income countries which are identical in other attributes. When Dy_t is expressed in percentage points, and y_t in logarithms, the absolute value of the coefficient on y_t gives the estimated annual percentage decrease in the income gap between the two countries. A positive relationship between human capital and economic growth emerges from expanded models of growth which include physical and human capital; in these models, the growth rate is generally increasing in the ratio of human to physical capital, with the empirical implication that Dy_t should be increasing in h_t, controlling for y_t.

The various control variables in the vector A can be interpreted as influences on either the level of technology or the rate of technological change. A wide variety of variables have been proposed for A. In an early and influential test of robustness, Levine and Renelt (1992) find that the investment-GDP ratio, the level of human capital (as measured by secondary school enrollment) and the initial level of per capita income are robust determinants of economic growth. Since then, a large number of other potential influence on economic growth have been identified, using broader criteria for robustness (Sala-I-Martin, 1997; USITC, 1997). Of these, we focus on two. Many studies have identified a measure of economic policy conducive to market activity, such as an index of the 'rule of law', 'institutional quality', 'economic freedom', or 'openness', to be positively correlated with economic growth. There appears to be substantial overlap among these concepts. We utilize the measure of openness to international economic activity developed by Sachs and Warner (1995), cumulated over intervals of time. Additionally, there is some evidence that the share of foreign direct investment (FDI) in GDP is positively associated with economic growth (Balasubramanyan et al., 1996), suggesting that a dollar of FDI is on the margin more beneficial than a dollar of domestically financed investment. This finding is consistent with the idea that FDI generally comes bundled with imported technology which is superior to domestic technology, thus providing the rationale for foreign investment in the first place. We include a measure of net FDI/GDP in our sample.[1]

This gives us our primary empirical specification as

$$Dy_{i,t} = \alpha + \beta_0 \ln(y_{i,t-1}) + \beta_1 h_{i,t} + \beta_2 I/Y_{i,t} + \beta_3 FDI/Y_{i,t} + \beta_4 OPEN_{i,t} + \varepsilon_{i,t}$$

in which I indexes countries, t indexes time, and α and the β's are coefficients to be estimated. The marginal effect of either export specialization (SPECL) or export structural change is then examined by adding one or the other of these variables in a linear fashion to the above specification.

Our data consist of observations on countries over five-year intervals, beginning in 1961-1965 and ending in 1991-1995. Observations for most of the variables are averaged over these 5-year intervals. The initial level of income, $\ln(y_{i,t-1})$, for, e.g. 1991-1995 is measured in 1990, and the corresponding $Dy_{i,t}$ is the annualized 5-year growth rate calculated using 1990 and 1995 as reference points.[2] We use secondary school enrollment, as per World Bank data, and with some interpolation, as our measure of human capital. Dy, h, I/Y and FDI/Y are expressed in percentage terms for convenience. OPEN is the sum of the Sachs-Warner variable over 5-year intervals, so that a value of 0 indicates that the country pursued closed policies throughout the interval while a value of 5 indicates that the country was consistently open. Since episodes of opening and closing take place mid-interval, OPEN exhibits sufficient variation to be usable in a fixed-effects specification.

The use of panel data for estimation of the canonical growth equation has been explored by Islam (1995). The case for using panel data consists primarily in the fact that the simplest neoclassical specification assumes constant labor productivity across countries, with per capita income varying only due to differences in the capital/labor ratio, whereas in reality levels of productivity vary widely across countries. These variations in productivity can be captured by permitting α to vary across countries. The most common techniques for doing this are the fixed-effects, or least-squares dummy variables, estimator, and the random-effects estimator. Expressing $Dy_{i,t}$ as $\ln(y_{i,t}) - \ln(y_{i,t-1})$, and rearranging terms, the above regression can be rewritten as a regression of $\ln(y_{i,t})$ on $\ln(y_{i,t-1})$ and other variables. In the presence of a lagged dependent variable, the fixed-effects estimator unfortunately is inconsistent asymptotically as $N \rightarrow \infty$ (but fortunately consistent as $T \rightarrow \infty$). The random-effects estimator suffers the more serious drawback that the country productivity effects must be assumed uncorrelated with the other variables in the model, and this appears highly unlikely. Thus, we proceed on the basis of the fixed-effects estimator.[3]

In order to investigate the possibility that our results on Latin American export specialization and structural changed may be influenced by anomalies in the other parameters of a growth equation estimated solely on Latin American data, we also took subsamples of data for sub-Saharan Africa and developing Asia, for which we had measures of all the variables of interest except export specialization and export structural change. Each of these samples was selected on countries classified by the World Bank as 'developing' in both the initial and terminal year; the practical effect of this is that the developing Asia example excludes Hong Kong, likely an outlier in any event. The characteristics of these three subsamples, and of the pooled sample, are described in Table 7.2. There are only about half as many observations for developing Asia as for the other two regions. Measured at the mean, the developing Asia subsample exhibits the highest rate of per capita GDP growth, of investment/GDP, of secondary school enrollment/GDP, and of openness. The sub-Saharan Africa sample shows the slowest growth, and lowest levels of secondary school enrollment, openness, and initial per capita income. The ratio of FDI to GDP is similar in all three samples, and the aggregate rate of investment is only moderately higher in aggregate in developing Asia than in Latin America, where it is the lowest. Of the three subsamples, the Latin American subsample is most nearly similar to the pooled total sample, except for higher initial levels of per capita income, and would be expected to show features similar to a standard cross-country analysis of developing countries.

Results

The results of initial OLS estimation on the full sample and on the three subsamples, using the common set of variables, are reported in Table 7.3, with the corresponding fixed-effects estimates in Table 7.4. Estimates are presented both with and without secondary school enrollment; omission of secondary school enrollment increases somewhat the available degrees of freedom due to missing observations on the variable. The coefficients on secondary school enrollment are in the main insignificant or perversely negative, both in OLS and in the fixed-effects specifications. This result, though seemingly unusual, replicates that in Islam (1995, Table V), with different subsamples, and using the human capital measure of Barro and Lee (1993). Similar results on the growth effects of human capital over multiple time periods are found by De Gregorio (1992). While human capital is usually a positive determinant of growth in a single cross section, in which the dependent variable is an annualized growth rate over 25 - 40 years, it ceases to appear as so in a panel sample, where each country is observed over several time periods, whether or not the panel aspect of the data is specifically treated econometrically. An intuition behind this result is that while education indeed does matter, observed levels of school enrollment or other measures of human capital have tended gradually upwards over time in most countries. Thus, a finding of a positive coefficient of human capital on per capita income growth in a panel sample would imply that per capita income growth tends to accelerate over time, which it does not.

Otherwise, the standard results are fairly robust across regions in terms of sign, though the magnitudes of the coefficients varies across regions. Employing an appropriate panel estimator increases the estimated rate of convergence in the pooled sample and in all regions except developing Asia, and increases the estimated growth effects of investment in the pooled sample and in all regions except sub-Saharan Africa, while the estimated effects of FDI are lower under fixed effects. Given that a dollar's worth of FDI increases both FDI/GDP and investment/GDP, the significant positive sign for FDI in the fixed-effects estimates for the pooled sample, Latin America, and developing Asia reinforces the idea that the growth effects of a dollar of FDI exceed those of a dollar of domestically financed investment. The coefficient for openness is modestly lower in the pooled sample estimated under fixed effects than in the same sample estimated under OLS, and varies markedly across regions, presumably because of differences in the distribution of the openness variable. The effects of openness are easiest to detect within sub-Saharan Africa, where relatively few countries are open, and in the pooled sample including sub-Saharan Africa.

Table 7.5 summarizes the differences in estimates across regions, comparing the coefficients using a standard difference-of-means test for samples with unequal variances (Hogg and Tanis, 1977, p. 252), and using the specifications excluding secondary-school enrollment. The effect of investment on economic growth is highest in the Latin America subsample, middling in the developing Asia subsample, and lowest in the sub-Saharan Africa subsample, implying a similar ranking of the marginal product of capital in the three regions. The growth effect of FDI is unambiguously higher in Latin America than in sub-Saharan Africa. In the OLS specification the returns to FDI are overall highest in Latin America, while introduction of country-specificfixed effects yields the largest FDI returns in developing Asia. The rate of convergence is unambiguously highest (i.e. the sign of the coefficient on initial per capita income is unambiguously lowest) in Latin America, again suggesting that the regional marginal product of capital is higher in Latin America than in the other two regions. Convergence appears slowest in sub-Saharan Africa under the OLS estimates, while under fixed effects Asian convergence appears slowest. Here the fixed-effects result, preferable on econometric grounds, is also consistent with the idea that high rates of savings and investment in Asia would have led to lower returns on the margin, though the coefficient on the investment/GDP ratio does not provide the same result. On openness, while the OLS results indicate significant differences across regions in the effects of openness on growth, the fixed-effects estimates fail to reject the null hypothesis that the coefficient in the three subsamples is equal.

From this exercise we can conclude that although the parameters of the aggregate production function probably do differ across regions, particularly the parameters of variables shifting the A(.) function for labor productivity, the determinants of growth in Latin America are sufficiently typical that examination of the growth effects of export specialization and export structural change in a sample restricted to Latin America may not be unduly influenced by peculiarities of the Latin American growth process in general. Table 7.6, then, adds to the specification the variables for export specialization and export structural change, one at a time. In the preferred fixed-effects specification, export specialization is significantly negatively correlated with per capita income growth (i.e. export *diversification* is positively correlated with growth, after controlling for other likely determinants of economic growth. The cautions voice by McCloskey (1985, chapter Nine) on the uses of statistical significance in economic rhetoric are of particular relevance here. (In fact, they have been relevant throughout the discussion, but it is particularly handy to introduce these here, at the climax of our argument). First, we are dealing with a sample of nineteen countries that represent well over 90 percent of Latin American economic activity; there is no 'universe' of thousands of hypothetical Latin American countries which is sampled here. Thus, the estimates obtained by the regression model really do characterize economic activity in Latin America over 1960-1995 regardless of whether any individual coefficient is 'significant' in the sense of the Neymann-Pearson classical sampling paradigm, which is the sense in which t-statistics and their p-values are to be taken, if taken literally. What is of primary interest is whether the coefficients are economically 'important' in the sense that interesting-sized movements in the independent variablesproduce movements of equally practical interest in the dependent variable.

Table 7.2 Means of Variables by Subsample

	Full Sample	Latin America	Sub-Saharan Africa	Developing Asia
Per capita GDP growth	1.23	0.90	0.55	3.16
Gross fixed investment/GDP	20.6	19.3	20.7	23.0
Foreign direct investment/GDP	1.24	1.28	1.22	1.21
Secondary school enrollment	32.3	39.8	15.4	45.6
log(initial per capita income)	6.62	7.23	6.12	6.38
Openness (Sachs-Warner)	1.40	1.53	0.87	2.17
Export specialization		0.316		
Export structural change		0.0312		
N	290	115	115	60
N (for secondary school enrollment)	259	110	93	56

Table 7.3 Growth Equation Estimates - Ordinary Least Squares

	Full Sample	Full Sample	Latin America	Latin America	Sub-Saharan Africa	Sub-Saharan Africa	Developing Asia	Developing Asia
Intercept	2.71	1.93	9.34	10.6	2.63	0.624	5.28	4.80
	(2.18)**	(1.67)*	(2.39)**	(3.40)**	(1.23)	(0.32)	(1.93)*	(1.92)*
Gross fixed	0.133	0.118	0.190	0.184	0.125	0.0973	0.169	0.170
investment/GDP	(5.88)***	(6.19)***	(3.28)***	(3.40)***	(4.29)***	(4.21)***	(2.80)***	(3.06)***
Foreign direct	0.261	0.250	0.394	0.406	0.243	0.276	0.108	0.0526
investment/GDP	(3.97)***	(3.87)***	(2.72)***	(3.03)***	(3.20)***	(3.69)***	(0.45)	(0.002)
Secondary school	0.938		-1.15		-3.91		0.716	
enrollment	(1.18)		(0.69)		(2.09)**		(0.42)	
log(initial per capita	-0.788	-0.583	-1.70	-1.92	-0.760	-0.425	-1.07	-0.957
income)	(4.00)***	(3.37)***	(2.74)***	(4.14)***	(2.12)**	(1.30)	(2.24)**	(2.29)**
Openness (Sachs-	0.330	0.302	0.121	0.0669	0.400	0.208	0.226	0.256
Warner)	(4.50)***	(4.38)***	(1.06)	(0.66)	(2.68)***	(1.56)	(1.46)	(1.75)*
N	259	290	110	115	93	115	56	60
R^2	0.290	0.247	0.256	0.243	0.368	0.274	0.296	0.291
Mean of dependent variable	1.28	1.23	0.89	0.90	0.56	0.56	3.23	3.16

T- statistics in parentheses. *** - significant at .01 ** - significant at .05 * - significant at .10

Dependent variable is growth rate of per capita income. All data are averaged over five-year periods, beginning in 1961-65 and ending in 1991-95.

Table 7.4 Growth Equation Estimates -Fixed Effects

	Full Sample	Full Sample	Latin America	Latin America	Sub-Saharan Africa	Sub-Saharan Africa	Developing Asia	Developing Asia
Gross fixed investment/GDP	0.192 (6.56)***	0.161 (6.81)***	0.256 (4.45)***	0.246 (4.53)***	0.175 (4.23)***	0.141 (4.79)***	0.276 (0.37)	0.273 (0.38)
Foreign direct investment/GDP	0.121 (1.76)*	0133 (1.98)**	0.280 (1.71)*	0.335 (2.20)**	0.00765 (0.09)	-.0124 (0.15)	0.710 (2.44)**	0.659 (2.30)**
Secondary school enrollment	-3.29 (2.15)**		-1.68 (0.72)		-3.06 (1.08)		-0.456 (0.13)	
log(initial per capita income)	-3.21 (5.10)***	-4.00 (7.63)***	-6.17 (5.11)***	-6.58 (7.03)***	-4.16 (3.72)***	-5.32 (5.49)***	-0.792 (0.68)	-0.873 (0.95)
Openness (Sachs-Warner)	0.275 (3.32)***	0.203 (2.64)**	0.184 (1.77)*	0.153 (1.61)	0.316 (1.68)*	0.159 (1.06)	0.140 (0.60)	0.148 (0.70)
N	259	290	110	115	93	115	56	60
R^2	0.267	0.258	0.448	0.440	0.257	0.294	0.148	0.128
Mean of dependent variable	1.28	1.23	0.89	0.90	0.56	0.56	3.23	3.16

T- statistics in parentheses. *** - significant at .01 ** - significant at .05 * - significant at .10

Dependent variable is growth rate of per capita income. All data are averaged over five-year periods, beginning in 1961-65 and ending in 1991-95.

Table 7.5 Difference-of-Means Tests Across Regions (specifications without secondary school enrollment, export specialization, or export structural change)

	Latin America vs. Sub-Saharan Africa		Latin America vs. Developing Asia		Sub-Saharan Africa vs. Developing Asia	
	OLS	Country fixed eff.	OLS	Country fixed eff.	OLS	Country fixed eff.
Investment						
Test statistic	15.77	17.59	1.56	20.64	-9.65	-3.67
p-value	1	1	0.94	1	0	0.0001
Foreign dir. investment						
Test statistic	9.04	20.82	13.06	-8.14	9.42	-0.43
p-value	1	1	1	1.94e-16	1	0.33
Convergence						
Test statistic	-28.10	-1.25	-13.8	-38.45	8.52	-4.31
p-value	0	0.106	0	0	1	0
Openness						
Test statistic	-8.981	-0.365	-8.88	0.17	-2.09	0.35
p-value	1.36e-19	0.36	3.25e-19	0.56	0.018	0.638

The estimated coefficient on export specialization is in this sense both statistically significant and economically important. The fixed-effects estimate, of -3.96, implies that the difference in annual per capita income growth between a highly diversified exporter (e.g. Argentina in the early 1990s, as per Table 7.1) and a highly specialized exporter (e.g. Venezuela, in the same period) is on the order of $(3.96)(0.725-0.021) \approx 2.8$ percent per year, a very substantial amount. Even the smaller and not conventionally significant estimate from OLS implies a difference in growth rates of $(0.911)(0.725-0.021) \approx 0.65$ percent per year, still a fairly striking amount.

The negative sign for our export structural change variable suggests that structural change is, *ceteris paribus*, associated with weaker economic growth; however, in neither the OLS nor the fixed-effects estimates does the result achieve standard levels of statistical significance. Recall that in earlier work on annual time series data, referenced above, we obtained a similar result for Chile but obtained the reverse result for Colombia, and that in eye balling the long-run relationship between export structural change and growth, structural change appeared to be positively, if weakly, associated with stronger economic growth. The regression results might be given some weight in resolving this ambiguity, even failing the standard. As a measure of economic importance, one can use the difference between the peak country average structural change value of 0.0379 centered on 1978 and the low country average value of 0.0207

Table 7.6 Latin America - Results With Export Specialization and Export Structural Change

	OLS	OLS	Fixed effects	Fixed effects
Intercept	10.2 (3.25)***	11.9 (3.63)***	NA	NA
Gross fixed investment/GDP	0.184 (3.39)***	0.186 (3.45)***	0.266 (4.90)***	0.246 (4.50)***
Foreign direct investment/GDP	0.432 (3.15)***	0.378 (2.79)***	0.339 (2.26)**	0.334 (2.13)**
log(initial per capita income)	-1.83 (3.86)***	-2.02 (4.31)***	-7.44 (7.38)***	-6.58 (6.97)***
Openness (Sachs-Warner)	0.0584 (0.57)	0.834 (0.82)	0.108 (1.12)	0.153 (1.59)
Export specialization	-0.911 (0.87)		-3.96 (2.11)**	
Export structural change		-18.3 (1.26)		-0.251 (0.18)
N	115	115	115	115
R^2	0.249	0.254	0.462	0.440
Mean of dependent variable	0.90	0.90	0.90	0.90

T- statistics in parentheses. *** - significant at .01 ** - significant at .05 * - significant at .10

centered on 1988 to exemplify the difference between periods of rapid and slow export structural change. Using the OLS estimates, a period of more rapid structural change is associated with a slowdown of (18.3)(0.0379-0.0207) ≈ 0.3 percent per annum in per capita economic growth, not trivial, but not big enough to associate with recession or deep crisis in general. Using the presumably preferable estimates from the fixed effects procedure,one finds the difference between rapid and low structural change associated with a reduction of (0.251)(0.0379-0.0286) ≈ 0.004 percent per annum, which is negligible. This result leads us to fall back on the insight arising from comparing the Dependent variable is growth rate of per capita income. All data are averaged over five-year periods, beginning in 1961-1965 and ending in 1991-1995. country studies, namely that an acceleration of export structural change can be associated in practice with either economic expansion or contraction, with the mechanisms underlying periods of structural change being country-specific. A strengthened emphasis on the traditional primary product can be associated either with health or stagnation, and a search for new products with either Schumpeterian crisis or Schumpeterian renewal.[4]

Conclusion

The primary points arising from the foregoing analysis, and immediate inferences from these points, are as follows:

- There has been a long-run trend toward export diversification in Latin America since the early 1960s; while this trend has accelerated and decelerated, it has never reversed for any substantial period of time. Using a standard empirical framework for analyzing economic growth with panel data, we find that Latin American countries with relatively diversified exports grow faster than those with relatively specialized exports. The potential effect of export diversification on economic growth appears large enough to account for a good portion of differences in cross-country growth performance in the region.
- The average rate of structural change in export composition in Latin America has undergone long swings, on the order of 20-25 years from peak to trough, with significant differences among countries. There is no readily

achievable generalization about the relationship between export structural change and economic growth.

- The underlying determinants of economic growth in Latin America are broadly similar to those for developing countries as a whole; thus, the positive association we find between export diversification and economic growth in Latin America is unlikely to be induced by regional peculiarities. It would be useful to discover whether this association is replicated for other regions, for a broader sample of developed countries, or for developing countries.
- In comparisons of growth empirics across regions, we find that within the broad similarity between the determinants of growth in Latin America, sub-Saharan Africa, and developing Asia, Latin America experiences relatively large growth effects from increases in investment in general and in direct investment in particular. Furthermore, the rate of convergence between poorer and richer countries is more rapid in Latin America than in other developing regions. These results taken together suggest that the marginal return on investment has been relatively high in Latin America compared to other developing regions, and that the region should over the long run experience a continued ability both to attract foreign capital and to retain domestic savings.

Notes

1. Since our sample consists of countries which were still classified as developing as of 1995, net and gross foreign domestic investment are approximately equal in most cases. A sample including developed countries, or economies such as Hong Kong and Singapore, would more appropriately utilize a variable for gross (inbound) FDI.
2. We use contemporaneous human capital, rather than lagged human capital, due to the lack of data from the late 1950s. Because of the behavior of the human capital variable, this makes relatively little difference for the results. For export structural change, we use the value centered on the 5-year period, e.g. the 1983 value, which utilizes export data from 1980-1986, is used to characterise the 1981-1985 interval. Because of truncation at both ends of the data, we matched the 1965 value (using 1962-68 data) to the observation for 1961-1965, and the 1992 value (using 1989-1995 data) for the 1991-1995 observation. Re-estimating our equations omitting the initial and/or terminal periods yielded results qualitatively similar to those presented here; thus, we report estimates using the full sample.

3. Islam (1995), in a Monte Carlo study based on his growth regression data, found that a fixed-effects estimator, while performing 'very well', was surpassed by Chamberlin's Minimum Distance estimator, but that actual estimation results using the two were very similar.
4. However, see the recent results of Kose (1998), who finds, using variance decomposition methods, that price shocks of primary commodities relative to prices of capital goods and intermediate inputs explain about 75 percent of business cycle variation in small open economies. If accelerated structural change in exports is associated with periods of relative price instability between various tradable goods, then a deeper analysis may potentially identify an underlying mechanism linking export structural change with fluctuations in economic growth.

References

Amin Gutiérrez de Piñeres, Sheila and Michael J. Ferrantino (1997a), 'Export Diversification and Structural Change: Some Comparisons for Latin America', *The International Executive*, vol. 39, no. 4, July/August, 465-477.

Amin Gutiérrez de Piñeres, Sheila and Michael J. Ferrantino (1997b), 'Export Diversification and Structural Dynamics in the Growth Process: The Case of Chile', *Journal of Development Economics*, Vol. 52, No. 2, April, 375-391.

Amin Gutiérrez de Piñeres, Sheila and Michael J. Ferrantino (1999), 'Export Sector Dynamics and Economic Growth: The Case of Colombia', *Review of Development Economics,* October, vol. 3, no.3, pp. 268-280.

Amin Gutiérrez de Piñeres, Sheila and Michael J. Ferrantino (forthcoming), 'The Commodity Composition of Export Portfolios: A Comparative Analysis of Latin America', *Latin American Business Review.*

Balasubramanyan, V.N., M.A. Salisu and D. Sapsford (1996), 'Foreign Direct Investment and Growth in EP and IS Countries', *The Economic Journal*, Vol. 106, pp. 92-105.

Barro, Robert and Xavier Sala-I-Martin (1995), *Economic Growth*, New York: McGraw-Hill.

Chua, Hak B. (1993), 'Regional Spillovers and Economic Growth', *Yale University Economic Growth Center Discussion Paper* no. 700 (September), New Haven: Yale University.

De Gregorio, Jose (1992), 'Economic Growth in Latin America', *Journal of Development Economics*, Vol. 39, 59-84.

Hogg, Robert V. and Elliot A. Tanis (1977), *Probability and Statistical Inference*, New York: Macmillan.

Islam, Nazrul (1995), 'Growth Empirics: A Panel Data Approach', *Quarterly Journal of Economics*, Vol. 110, No. 4 (November), 1127-1170.

Kose, M. Ayhan (1998), 'Explaining Business Cycles in Small Open Economies: How Much Do World Prices Matter?', Brandeis University, processed.

Levine, Ross, and David Renelt (1992), 'A Sensitivity Analysis of Cross-Country Growth Regressions', *American Economic Review*, Vol. 82, No. 4 (September), 942-963.

McCloskey, Donald N. (1985), *The Rhetoric of Economics,* Madison: University of Wisconsin Press.

Sachs, Jeffrey and Andrew Warner (1995), 'Economic Reform and the Process of Integration,' *Brookings Papers on Economic Activity*, 1995:1, 1-118.

Sala-I-Martin, Xavier (1997), 'I Just Ran Two Million Regressions', *American Economic Review*, Vol. 87, No. 2 (May), 178-183.

U.S. International Trade Commission (1997), *The Dynamic Effects of Trade Liberalization: An Empirical Analysis*, publication 3069 (October); Washington, DC: USITC.

8 Externalities in the Export Sector and Economic Growth*

Introduction

Many prominent agricultural economists such as Irma Adelman (1995b) have recognized the value and important role of agriculture in development. Adelman (1995b), however, focuses on agricultural-demand-led industrialization (ADLI). ADLI focuses on shifting a greater share of domestic resources and investment into the agricultural sector than a purely export led strategy. The emphasis is on the small and medium scale farmer and increased agricultural productivity and the linkages provided by higher rural incomes. ADLI supports an open economy that leads to a more efficient allocation of resources since prices are no longer distorted. The ideas proposed in this paper differ from ADLI in that they emphasize the important and dynamic role of agricultural exports for economic growth. The model, in this paper, was developed to extend the commonly held belief that the agricultural sector could only affect long run growth rates through increased demand for manufactured goods or that the only road to development is through industrialization and manufacturing.

The externalities of agricultural led growth are many. Adelman and Robinson(1995a) point out that others such as Frank and Webb (1977), Stewart and Streeten (1971), and Chenery et al. (1974) 'suggest that certain changes in emphasis-for example, a shift to more labor-intensive technologies, to export promotion in trade policy, to rural rather than industrial development, or a broad based, skill-intensive growth strategy-might favor more equality and need not hinder rapid growth'. Adelman (1995b) suggests that an agricultural

---

* This chapter is reprinted in parts from Amin Gutiérrez De Piñeres, Sheila, 'Externalities in the Export Sector and Long Run Growth Rates', *Singapore Economic Review*, vol. 41, no. 1 (April, 1996), pp. 13-24 and Amin Gutiérrez De Piñeres, Sheila, 'Externalities in the Agricultural Export Sector and Economic Growth: A Developing Country Perspective', *Agricultural Economics*, vol 21, (1999) pp 257-267.

development program is more labor intensive than even labor intensive manufacturing. While traditional agriculturalhas its place in development, this paper addresses the value of nontraditional agriculture in development and its potential role as an engine of growth. Nontraditional agriculture in many cases requires a complex infrastructure and significant human capital investment before it can succeed; and, therefore should not be ignored in the policy agenda of developing countries. In the case of Colombia, for example, the agricultural sector in its own right increased Colombia's GNP with fresh cut flower exports being Colombia's fourth largest export and fresh horticulture exports growing rapidly (UNCTAD,1998).

To date endogenous growth models have identified human capital (knowledge) in a general sense as a source of growth (Lucas, 1988; Romer, 1990). In the model developed here it is only human capital in export sector that has the potential to increase growth rates. Given that in many developing countries human capital is limited, it should be utilized in sectors that have the most potential to add to the knowledge base, and consequently increase long run growth rates.

Research expended in the import competing sector will be considered redundant, while research in the export sector will be considered original research. Research is defined as the search to improve production efficiency, infrastructure, and/or knowledge. Research in the import competing sector is redundant because the goods could just be imported avoiding costly research, and human capital expenditures, in developing the good at home. Research in the export sector is considered original because it adds to country specific knowledge and leads to the growth of similar and interrelated industries.

However, it has been documented that research in the import competing sector does add to the stock of knowledge in the sense that minor innovations are made to adapt the foreign technology to domestic factors. For example, Katrak (1989) showed that in India imports increased the likelihood that an enterprise would commence R&D activity. The initial increase in R&D may be because the 'imported technology must be adapted to local environments. But adaptive activity may not be the only type of effort induced by the imported technology. In fact, the experience gained through adaptive effort may enable enterprises to respond to other needs for R&D: for instance ... to undertake minor innovations'(Katrak,1989, p.124). This is further supported by the results of Sebastien Dessus (1999) as he posits that 'the significant contribution of imported intermediate inputs to TFP growth could reflect the fact that copying and 'reverse engineering' of a broad range of foreign products was a valuable source of technological learning and improvement during the earlier period of Taiwan's industrialization'. In this paper, the focus is on the benefits from research in the export sector, which utilizes imported intermediate goods.

The model in this paper considers how the externalities of research devoted to the export sector as opposed to the import-competing sector affect long run growth rates. Research is defined as the search to improve production efficiency, infrastructure, and/or knowledge. Research expended in the import competing sector will be defined as redundant, while research in the export sector will be considered original. Research in the import-competing sector is redundant because the goods could just be imported, avoiding costly research in developing the good at home. Research in the export sector is considered original because it adds to country specific knowledge and leads to the growth of other industries. The export sector is divided into two subsectors to capture the externality.

The focus, of this paper, is on developing countries whose comparative advantage lies in the labor intensive agricultural sector. However, the analysis of the model can also be applied to countries that began by exporting high technology goods and are now branching out into highly perishable agricultural exports, like Taiwan and Malaysia. Since most developing countries have a shortage of human capital the goal should be to avoid redundant research.

The representative agent growth model in this paper contains an application to the Colombian economy in that it identifies the source of the growth as knowledge generated by human capital investment in an export sector, the flower industry. Human capital investment in the flower export sector has positive externalities; the country's knowledge base increases resulting in the growth of similar industries, such as the fruit and vegetable sectors. Research is separated into the import-competing and export sectors. The export sector is divided into two subsectors, proxying the flower and fruit/vegetable sectors, to capture the interplay of knowledge between the two nontraditional export sectors.

Export Promotion as a Source of Growth

There are growth theory models that consider export promotion as a source of growth (Edwards 1993); however, it is not the human capital investment in the export sector that is the driving force behind growth in these models. The rationale for considering exports 'is based on a possible positive externality and technological diffusion effects generated by more rapid exports' (Edwards 1993). Empirically, experiments by countries in import substitution have been dismal failures. Given the results of India's and many Latin American countries' import substitution policies, the 'tide seems to have turned in the favor of export oriented policies. Export promotion creates incentives for entrepreneurship, productivity, and thrift' (Lal and Rajapatirana 1987). Lal and Rajapatirana's (1987) survey of the literature on trade as an engine of growth concludes trade induces growth only in the sense it limits the government.

Lewis (1955), however, argues that developing countries that are more integrated with the world have an advantage in technology generated in the advanced countries. Another of the justifications for export promotion is that it moves a country on to its production possibilities frontier by equating international to domestic marginal rate of transformation (Krueger, 1980). Another is that trade allows an industry to capture the benefits of a larger market; i.e. increasing returns to scale, efficient plant size, and other indivisibilities in the production process. Chen and Tang (1987) conducted an empirical study of the technical efficiency of import-competing and export-oriented firms in Taiwan. They use data from an annual survey of foreign firms by the Taiwanese government in 1980. The firms are separated into import-competing and export-oriented firms. They conclude that export-oriented firms tend to be six to eleven percent closer to the production frontier than import-substitution oriented firms (Chen and Tang, 1987). The exact degree to which the firms are closer to the production function frontier depends on the specification of the model.

Edwards (1993) has done some initial empirical work on the absorption rate of technological advances and growth. Edwards considers a small developing country that faces given world prices and innovations that are developed in advanced countries. Given these proxies and other variables, Edwards finds that outward orientation and export growth have positive impacts on income growth.

Recent theoretical work on the importance of an open trade policy has been done by Rivera-Batiz and Romer (1991a, 1991b). They have developed various models focusing on the fact that trade restrictions can possibly impede the free flow of knowledge, and consequently decrease world wide growth rates. Their models are one sector growth models that focus on two similar developed countries. World wide integration allows the countries to capture the increasing returns to scale in the research and development sector (Rivera-Batiz, 1991a). Additionally, a substantial amount of empirical research has been done on the externalities of knowledge and learning by doing in the export sector. This research has focused, however, on the micro-level and the interplay between these externalities at the firm level. Aitken et al. (1997), examine the question of whether firms that enter foreign markets reduce entry costs for other potential exports through learning effects or establishing commercial linkages. They find that export spillovers are restricted to multinational activity (p.128) In their case examining the Mexican manufacturing sector, foreign firms provided a 'catalyst' for domestic firms to export. Using data from the Colombian manufacturing sector, Roberts and Tybout (1997) find that prior exporting experience significantly affects current decision to export but it quickly depreciates over time. They also find evidence that export infrastructure such as trading companies and distribution agents are important. Another study by Clerrides et al.(1996), using manufacturing data from Colombia, Mexico, and Morocco indicates that there is some evidence to support the finding that exporters reduce the costs of breaking into foreign markets for domestically oriented producers. Developing countries' comparative advantage lies in their agricultural sector and large pool of unskilled and semi-skilled labor; yet, none of these studies approach the agricultural sector or examine externalities related to it. This paper moves this research one step further by developing a model that illustrates externalities in the agricultural export sector and applies the model to Colombia.

An Application to Colombia

Colombia has a natural comparative advantage in growing and exporting fresh cut flowers (Mendez, 1991) [henceforth fresh cut flowers will be referred to as flowers]. The climate and luminosity conditions around the Savanna of Bogotá are ideal for growing flowers. Around the Savanna of Bogotá variations in temperature and humidity are minimal. This imparts a tremendous cost advantage since greenhouses do not have to be enclosed, nor do they require temperature and humidity controls. Natural growing conditions, including light, water, and soil, allow flowers to be grown year round (Lochhead, 1997). Additionally, it has a cheap supply of labor and is close to the American market. The flower industry is Colombia's second largest employer, providing some 75,00 direct and perhaps 50,00 more indirect ones (The Economist, 1993).

Flower exports by Colombia have been increasing since 1960, and by 1995 flowers had become Colombia's fourth largest export. The flowers first grew around the plains of Bogotá but now have spread to areas in Colombia's mountainous Andean regions (Americas, 1990). From 1970 to 1980, flower exports increased ten-fold, to US $100 million, and then doubled again in the next eight years to reach US $206 million by the end of 1988, and by 1995 had increased to more than $500 million and continues to grow [see Table 8.1]. In the late 1970s, there were only 1,500 acres under floral cultivation; however, now there are 400 flower farms that cultivate more than 10,000 acres (Lennard, 1997). Colombia is now the world's largest exporter of carnations and second only to the Netherlands in world aggregate exports of flowers. Colombian growers are now expanding their markets by simultaneously introducing and marketing new types of flowers in the United States.

The government encouraged exports by not taxing inputs into the production process. In the case of flowers, the importation of the motherstock was essential to the growth of the industry. The motherstock and basic technology of the flower industries in Colombia were imported from Israel and Italy in the 1970s. In Colombia, under the *Vallejo Plan*, there are no tariffs on goods that are inputs into the production process of an export. However, the importer must pay royalties on the use of the motherstock. Thus, there are now laboratories in Colombia which are trying to propagate the motherstock to avoid these royalties. Most technology was imported and then adapted to the country's special characteristics. The imported technology was general knowledge regarding fertilizer and pesticide requirements, diseases and the treatment of these diseases. The irrigation systems used are now produced nationally as are the fertilizers and pesticides.

Flowers are handled as highly perishable products. In essence, cut flowers are like fruits/vegetables and deteriorate through complex physiological processes (Hardenburg, 1990). Flowers must be monitored and handled with knowledge from the farm to the consumer. Selling flowers requires a substantial investment in infrastructure which includes both physical and human capital. The process by which flowers are imported and sold in the United States is as follows: 'the flower farms sell the produce to an importer who ships the flowers into the U.S., usually through Miami or New York. The importers sell the flowers to wholesalers, which then sell to the retail shops. The process typically takes about a week, and can take as long as two weeks (Mollenkamp, 1999).' Since flowers are highly perishable and often only have a limited life, it is important that principals involved in the exporting process be educated as to the needs of the flowers.

Colombia is known for the high quality of its flowers (Deveny,1985). The flowers are treated with preservatives to extend shelf-life. The process for harvesting, treating, storing and packing flowers for export is intricate (Hardenburg, 1990). Human capital investment in the flower industry has been significant. Additionally, a well developed marketing system exists to distribute and sell the flowers once they are imported. Many of the marketing firms are Colombian owned which facilitates entry into the market by exporters of other perishable goods. This general knowledge base provides a basis for other exporters of highly perishables.

To illustrate the value of the spillover effects, in 1999 Dole Food Co. began to move into the fresh cut flower market by buying flower farms, and importing and marketing firms of flowers. In early 1999, Dole bought four of Colombia's largest and most successful flower growers, which account for about 25 percent of production (Rohter, 1999). Dole will bring to the Colombian flower industry its vast experience in growing, refrigeration, and distribution in perishables (Rohter, 1999). Aitken et al. (1997) found that spillovers from multinationals is significant in the manufacturing industry in Mexico. There is no reason to believe these spillovers do not also exist in the nontraditional agricultural sector.

Colombian tropical fruits earned almost 360 million US dollars in foreign exchange in 1989 (Colombia Today, 1990). Bananas, as always, have been the bulk of perishable exports, but other fruit exports have increased (see Table 8.1). The new fruits exported include pineapples, mangoes, lemons, figs, strawberries, melons, papayas, curubas, and passion fruit. The storage life of these fruits varies from 1-6 months for lemons to 5-7 days for strawberries and figs. Pineapples, mangoes, papayas, and passion fruits survive for approximately 2-4 weeks in storage. The export of fresh fruits such as figs and

Table 8.1 A Comparison of Flower and Fruit/Vegetable Exports
(Value in thousands of U.S. dollars)

Year	Flowers	Fruit/Vegetables*
1961	1	131
1965	20	348
1967		438
1968		911
1969		1226
1970	1000	1837
1971	1800	2889
1972	3100	3492
1973	8400	4933
1974	16000	13308
1975	19300	14980
1976	21600	11447
1977	32600	22222
1978	53400	21433
1979	79200	24572
1980	111837	113735
1981	123527	147557
1982	127108	177610
1983	134548	166527
1984	143011	213098
1985	148299	175046
1986	171212	228174
1987	160417	235577
1988	204989	278121
1989	240458	287016
1990	247280	359360
1991	300297	486097
1992	371008	453148
1993	408222	467987
1994	465917	530867
1995	517759	477100

* Excludes bananas

1961-1979 from UN data tapes: Flowers: SITC 29 (Crude Vegetable Matter) Fruits/Vegetables: SITC 05 (Fruits and Vegetables); 1980-1995 from STATS Canada: Flowers: SITC 2926 and 2927, 2926 bulbs, tubers and rhizomes of flowering or of foliage, 2927 cut flowers and foliage. Fruits/vegetables: SITC 0574+0575+0579+0586+0589, 0574 apples, fresh, 0575 grapes, fresh or dried, 0579 fruit,fresh or dried, n.e.s., 0586 fruit, temporarily preserved, 0589 fruit otherwise prepared or preserved, n.e.s.

strawberries requires a coordinated refrigeration system since they must be stored at 0°C with a relative humidity of 85 percent to 90 percent (Hardenburg, 1990). These conditions resemble those of the needs of flowers. Exporting flowers is more difficult than fruits and vegetables since they have a shorter shelf life, are more fragile, and require a clear protective packaging material (Kravetz, 1998). The potential for other industries to grow once the necessary infrastructure is in place is tremendous (Thomas, 1985). The infrastructure and knowledge base created by flower exports can be utilized by growers of other perishable products. With infrastructure being one of the most significant constraints to the growth of perishable exports, the expansion of the floral industry has had a positive impact on the export sector, especially those related to perishable goods (see Table 8.1).

Theoretical Model

The model, in this paper, outlines the effect of human capital in the export sector as opposed to the import competing sector on long run growth rates. The model is a representative agent model with three sectors, one import competing and two export sectors (proxied by the flower and fruit industries in Colombia); and three laws of motion for knowledge, wealth, and capital. The model is a continuous time optimizing problem which states that human capital in the export sector has a positive externality for the economy.

The model focuses on the externalities from the development of export oriented industries. The export sector is divided into two subsectors, export sector one, i.e. the flower sector in Colombia, and export sector two, fruit and vegetable sector in Colombia. The emphasis is on export sector one and how developments in this subsector can potentially facilitate the growth of export sector two. The knowledge gained by exporting goods produced in sector one can be utilized by other exporters. For example, in developing countries increases in exports of one good often lead to increased exports of other goods. In Chile, a variety of fresh fruits followed the export success of table grapes. In Colombia, fresh cut flowers were followed by highly perishable produce.

In this model, the economy produces an import substituting good [C_m] and two exportables: equivalent to export sector one [C_1] and export sector two [C_2]. The import competing good can be identified as the manufactured good. The agricultural sector can be identified as the main export sector for many developing countries. The import-competing good is produced domestically with the following production function: $M(K_m, L_m, H_m)$. The inputs are physical capital [K], labor [L], and human capital [H]. All physical capital [K_m] is imported so the question of effects of domestically producing capital goods is not considered.

The exportables are produced with the following production functions: $F(A, T_1, L_1, H_1)$ and $V(A, T_2, L_2, H_2)$. The export sector uses land [T] which is supplied inelastically, in addition to human capital [H], and labor [L]. The amount of land allocated to each subsector is fixed to simplify the math. The dynamics of the lag between planting a tree and production of the fruit are not considered in this model. It is assumed that once a fruit tree is planted it produces immediately. The export sector also has another input: knowledge [A] that is a by-product of human capital investment [H_1] in export sector one.

The source of growth, in the more recent endogenous growth models, has been specified by technologies that are functions of factors that can be accumulated without bound on a per capita basis (Romer 1992, Romer 1991, Romer 1990, Grossman and Helpman 1990 and 1991). One such factor that has received considerable attention is human capital formation (Lucas, 1988). Romer (1992) separated the process into human capital, which is bounded, and knowledge, which is a by-product of human capital and unbounded. Human capital is bounded because once an individual dies he/she takes his/her skills with him/her. Yet, the knowledge he/she contributed to society remains and is, therefore, unbounded and can be a source of growth and is described by a linear law of motion.

Available human capital is distributed between the three goods. The human capital investment in export sector one is assumed to produce a by-product that adds to the country's stock of country specific knowledge [A]. In the Colombian case, it is the knowledge on how to handle and market highly perishable flowers that can be used by other export industries to facilitate their expansion. Once the knowledge base on how to export exists other industries benefit from this externality. The law of motion for knowledge is:

$$\dot{A} = [\beta H_1]A$$

Knowledge is a function of the productivity factor [ß], human capital in export sector one [H_1], and existing country specific knowledge [A]. Human capital investment in the import competing sector [H_m] or export sector two [H_2] adds nothing to country specific knowledge [A]. The transfer of technology in this case is from export sector one to export sector two. In general it should not matter in which subsector the advancements are made as long as they are accessible to all the other sectors. However, to simplify the math only human capital in export sector one is included as part of the law of motion for knowledge.

The government's budget constraint is:

$$\pi^m[C_m - M] - \pi^1[F] - \pi^2[V] + \pi^i[I] = rb - \dot{b}$$

There are tariffs on imports of the consumption [π^m] and investment [π^i] goods. Investment is a function of new investment [I] and the capital stock [K]. There is also a tax [π^1,π^2 are negative] or subsidy [π^1,π^2 are positive] depending on the signs of π^1 and π^2 on the exportables. The agent can buy bonds [b] from the government. The government gets its revenue from import tariffs on the investment good and the import competing good. Additional revenue comes from the sale of bonds. The government can also collect money by taxing the exportable goods. Since it is assumed that there are no transfer payments, the government's only expense is to make interest payments on the bonds it has sold and/or subsidies on the exportables.

The representative agent's budget constraint is

$$\dot{b} = [(1+\pi^m)M + (1+\pi^1)F + (1+\pi^2)V] + rb - (1+\pi^m)C_m - (1+\pi^i)I$$

Goods produced in export sector one and export sector two are not consumed domestically; while the import competing good is. This consumption pattern is assumed because in general in a developing country when a commodity is successfully exported only non-export quality goods are left for domestic consumers. For example, only non-export quality flowers are sold domestically in Colombia (Americas, 1990). The sources of revenue for the representative agent are income from exporting sector one and two goods and interest earned on bonds purchased from the government. The agent spends his income on the investment good, consumption of the import competing good, and bonds.

The law of motion for capital is

$$\dot{K} = I - \theta K$$

The capital stock depreciates at a constant rate Θ. The representative agent maximizes utility subject to the agent's budget constraint, laws of motion for capital and knowledge and the fact that:

$$L = L_m + L_1 + L_2$$

$$K = K_m$$

$$H = H_m + H_1 + H_2$$

The utility function is assumed to be concave. The three goods are assumed to be normal goods. Labor supply and human capital are assumed to be fixed to reduce the number of state variables and make the mathematics more manageable. In this model, the representative agent recognizes the benefits of human capital investment in sector one when making his production decisions. If the agent failed to recognize the value of human capital in sector one to generate knowledge, the long run growth rate of the economy would be lower than optimal. The representative agent recognizes that investment in human capital export sector one yields positive externalities for the economy by increasing the country's knowledge base and internalizes this when maximizing his/her utility. Changes in the tariff and subsidy rates are exogenous.

The representative agent maximizes the following utility function:

$$\max \quad \int_0^{\infty} e^{-\delta t} U(C_{mt})$$

subject to the following constraints and the resource constraints identified above:

$$(\sigma) \quad \dot{b} = [(1+\pi^m)M + (1+\pi^1)F + (1+\pi^2)V] + rb - (1+\pi^m)C_m - (1+\pi^i)I$$

$$(\varphi) \quad \dot{A} = [\beta H_1]A$$

$$(\mu) \quad \dot{K} = I - \theta K$$

The shadow value of wealth, capital, and knowledge are σ, μ, and φ respectively.

The first order conditions are as follows (eq. 1 -6):

$$[C_m]: \ U'(C_m) - (1+\pi_m)\sigma = 0$$

$$[L_2]: \ (1+\pi^m)\sigma\frac{\partial M}{\partial L_2} + (1+\pi^2)\sigma\frac{\partial V}{\partial L_2} = 0$$

$$[L_1]: \ (1+\pi^m)\sigma\frac{\partial M}{\partial L_1} + (1+\pi^1)\sigma\frac{\partial F}{\partial L_1} = 0$$

$$[I]: \ -\sigma(1+\pi^i) + \mu = 0$$

$$[H_2]: \ (1+\pi^m)\sigma\frac{\partial M}{\partial H_2} + (1+\pi^2)\sigma\frac{\partial V}{\partial H_2} = 0$$

$$[H_1]: \ (1+\pi^m)\sigma\frac{\partial M}{\partial H_1} + (1+\pi^1)\sigma\frac{\partial F}{\partial H_1} + \beta A\varphi = 0$$

Equation (1) defines the usual intertemporal envelope condition that links the marginal utility of the consumption good to the shadow value of wealth. The equalization of the marginal product of labor across the three sectors seen in equations (2) and (3) is a consequence of the assumed mobility of labor. The link between the rate of accumulation of capital and the shadow value of capital is represented in equation (4). The value of human capital in export sector one (equation 6) consists of two parts: the direct marginal product and an indirect component due to the externality.

Additionally, the shadow value of wealth, capital, and knowledge evolve in accordance with the co-state equations. The co-state equations are (eq. 7-9):

$$\dot{\sigma} = \sigma(\delta - r)$$

$$\dot{\mu} = \mu(\theta + \delta) - \sigma(1+\pi^{m})\frac{\partial M}{\partial K}$$

$$\dot{\varphi} = \varphi(\delta - \beta H_1) - \sigma\left[(1+\pi^{1})\frac{\partial F}{\partial A} + (1+\pi^{2})\frac{\partial V}{\partial A}\right]$$

Given the production functions, first order conditions and co-state equations it is possible to solve for the relationship between the growth rate of the shadow value of wealth and the growth rate of consumption (eq. 10):

$$\frac{\dot{\sigma}}{\sigma} = -(\alpha)\frac{\dot{C}_m}{C_m}$$

where α is the coefficient of relative risk aversion. This assumes the utility function has the CRRA form. Equation (10) shows the relationship between the growth rate of the shadow value of wealth and the growth rate of consumption.

Given the marginal product of human capital across sectors is equalized, it is possible to solve for the shadow value of wealth [σ] (eq.11) using equations (6) and (5):

$$\sigma = \frac{\beta A\varphi}{\left[(1+\pi^{2})\frac{\partial V}{\partial H_2} - (1+\pi^{1})\frac{\partial F}{\partial H_1}\right]}$$

Substituting equation (11) into equation (9) solves for φ/φ, the rate of growth of the shadow value of knowledge (eq. 12):

$$\frac{\dot{\varphi}}{\varphi} = (\delta - \beta H_1) - \beta A\left[\frac{(1+\pi^2)\dfrac{\partial V}{\partial A} + (1+\pi^1)\dfrac{\partial F}{\partial A}}{(1+\pi^2)\dfrac{\partial V}{\partial H_2} - (1+\pi^1)\dfrac{\partial F}{\partial H_1}}\right]$$

The following relationships hold on the balanced growth path given the stock of human capital is fixed (eq. 13):

$$\frac{C_{\dot{m}}}{C_m} = \frac{\dot{A}}{A} \quad and \quad \frac{\dot{\sigma}}{\sigma} = \frac{\dot{\varphi}}{\varphi}$$

The rate of growth of consumption and knowledge must be equal along the balanced growth path for a given stock of labor and human capital.

Equation (13) coupled with equation (10) yields (eq. 14):

$$\frac{\dot{\varphi}}{\varphi} = (-\alpha)\frac{\dot{A}}{A}$$

The rate of growth of the shadow value of knowledge equals the rate of growth of knowledge times the coefficient of relative risk aversion on the balanced growth path.

Using equations (14), (12), and the law of motion for knowledge it is possible to solve for the long run growth rate:

$$-\alpha\beta H_1 = (\delta - \beta H_1) - \beta A\left[\frac{(1+\pi^2)\dfrac{\partial V}{\partial A} + (1+\pi^1)\dfrac{\partial F}{\partial A}}{(1+\pi^2)\dfrac{\partial V}{\partial H_2} - (1+\pi^1)\dfrac{\partial F}{\partial H_1}}\right]$$

To solve for the growth rate in terms of the initial parameters of the model, βH_1 must be isolated. Given the mathematical difficulty of this, only the effects of changes of the exogenously given subsidy and tariff rates on the long run growth rate can be determined (see Appendix for mathematical derivations). Since the agent does not choose the optimal level of subsidies, it can be determined how a change in the tariff or subsidy level will affect the path of long run growth rates.

The derivative of the long run growth rate with respect to a subsidy in export sector one is positive. If the subsidy to export sector one increases it has a positive affect on the long run growth rate. An increase in the subsidy drives human capital into export sector one as it expands. Since it is human capital in export sector one that adds to the country's stock of knowledge, an increase in human capital in export sector one will have a positive effect on the growth rate. However, it should be noted that the first best solution is to directly subsidize human capital in export sector one but since this is often politically infeasible the second best solution is to subsidize export sector one.

On the other hand, an increase in the subsidy to export sector two or an increase in tariffs in the import competing sector will have a negative effect on the growth rate. An increase in the subsidy to export sector two or tariffs in the import competing sector will drive human capital from export sector one into those sectors as they expand. This movement of human capital reduces the country's stock of knowledge since human capital in these sectors does not add to country specific knowledge. However, if policy changes result in human capital and resources moving solely between the import competing sector and export sector two the impact of these policy changes on the growth rate will be limited as human capital and resources in export sector one remain unchanged.

Conclusion

In the model developed in this paper, the premise is that only human capital in certain sectors has externalities and can be a source of growth. While increased levels of general human capital have social benefits for the economy, sector specific human capital has the potential to drive growth in an economy. In particular, human capital in the export sector is a source of externalities because it adds to country specific knowledge. In this case, human capital in a nontraditional agricultural export sector, the flower sector, is a source of knowledge. However, if the other sectors as defined in the model also contributed to the knowledge base there could come a point in time when they would have a larger impact on growth rates.

Since human capital tends to be limited in developing countries, it should be utilized in sectors where the country's comparative advantage lies. Human capital in the export sector can increase the country's comparative advantage allowing it to capture an even greater market share and wider market base. In the case of many developing countries it is the agricultural sector in which comparative advantage lies. In the Colombian example, expansion of the floral export sector had a significant impact on the expansion of highly perishable fruit and vegetable exports. Yet, too much of a good thing can be bad, a policy to shift all human capital into the flower sector would create an unsustainable equilibrium. Thus, while there may be a role for policy makers it is limited since long range foresight by policy makers often is hindered by their short run objectives. Given this, the second best policy prescription is a neutral one that does not favor any one sector but rather allows resources to move to the sector where the are valued the most.

The model in this paper reflects the value of export promotion and externalities in human capital to long run growth rates of developing countries. Export promotion shifts human capital into the export sector, traditionally the agricultural sector, and increases the possibilities for higher long run growth rates. The recent trend by policy makers to shift the negative bias of domestic and foreign policies away from the agricultural sector and move toward more neutral policies may provide additional evidence by which to test this model in the future.

References

Adelman, Irma (1995), 'Beyond Export-Led Growth', in Adelman, I. (Ed), *Institutions and Development Strategies: The Selected Essays of Irma Adelman*, Volume I, Edward Elgar, Brookfield, Vermont, pp.290-302.

Adelman, Irma, Bourniaux, Jean-Marc and Waelbroeck, Jean (1995), 'Agricultural Development-led Industrialisation in a Global Perspective', in Adelman, I. (Ed), *Institutions and Development Strategies: The Selected Essays of Irma Adelman*, Volume I, Edward Elgar, Brookfield, Vermont, pp.303-322.

Aitken, Brian, Hanson, Gordon and Harrison, Ann (1997), 'Spillovers, Foreign Investment, and Export Behavior', *Journal of International Economics*, vol. 43, pp. 103-132.

ASOCOLFLORES, various data bases, Bogota, Colombia.

Bloomberg News (1998), 'Dole Adds to Its Floral Arrangement', *The Los Angeles Times*, August 5, pp. 2.

Chen, Tain-jy and Tang, Depiao (1987), 'Comparing Technical Efficiency Between Import-Substitution- Oriented and Export-Oriented Foreign Firms in a Developing

Economy', *Journal of Development Economics*, vol. 26, pp. 277-289.

Chenery, Hollis, Ahluwalia, Montek, Bell, C.L.G., Duloy, J. and Jolly, R. (1974), *Redistribution with Growth,* Oxford, England: Oxford University Press.

Chenery, Hollis and Syrquin Moshe (1975), *Patterns of Development 1950-1970*, Oxford University Press: London.

Clerides, Sofronis, Saul, Lach and James Tybout (1998), 'Is Learning by Exporting Important? Micro- Dynamic Evidence from Colombia, Mexico and Morocco', *Quarterly Journal of Economics*, vol. 113, no.3, pp. 903-47.

Colombia Today (1990), 'Colombian Export Diversification. Colombia Information Service', vol.24, No.12.

Dessus, Sebastien (1999), 'Total Factor Productivity and Outward Orientation in Taiwan: What is the Nature of the Relationship', in Fu,T., Huang, C. and Lovell, A. (Eds), *Economic Efficiency and Productivity Growth in the Asia Pacific Region*, Edward Elgar: Brookfield, Vermont.

Deveny, Kathleen (1985), 'Now The Flower Business Is Blooming All Year', *Business Week*, (December 23) vol. 2926, pp. 59.

The Economist (1993). 'Colombian business-Fallow ground', (October 23) vol. 329, Issue 7834, p. 86.

Edwards, Sebastian (1993), 'Openness, Trade Liberalization, and Growth in Developing Countries', *Journal of Economic Literature*, vol. 31, pp. 1358-1393.

Elias, Victor (1985), 'Government Expenditures on Agriculture and Agricultural Growth in Latin America', International Food Policy Research Institute Research Report no. 50.

Frank, Charles, and Richard Webb, Eds. (1977), *Income Distribution: Policy Alternatives in Developing Countries,* Washington, D.C. Brookings Institution.

Grossman, Gene and Elhanan Helpman (1990), 'Comparative Advantage and Long Run Growth', *American Economic Review*, vol. 80, pp. 796-815.

Grossman, Gene and Elhanan Helpman (1991), 'Endogenous Product Cycles',*Economic Journal*, vol.101, pp. 1214-1229.

Hardenburg, R., Watada, A. and Wang, C. (1990), 'The Commercial Storage of Fruits, Vegetables, and Florist and Nursery Stocks', U.S. Department of Agriculture: Agriculture Handbook Number 66.

Katrak, Homi (1989), 'Imported Technologies and R&D in a Newly Industrializing Country: The Experience of Indian Enterprises', *Journal of Development Economics*, vol. 31, pp. 123-139.

Kravetz, Stacy (1998), 'Retailing: King of Pineapples Tiptoes to Tulips for Faster Growth', *Wall Street Journal,* (July 6) p. A17.

Krueger, Anne (1978), *Foreign Trade Regimes and Economic Development: Liberalization Attempts and Consequences*, Cambridge, MA: Ballinger Pub. Co. for NBER.

Lal,D. and Rajapatirana, S. (1987), 'Foreign Trade Regimes and Economic Growth in Developing Countries', *World Bank Research Observer* , vol 2, pp. 189-218.

Lennard, Jeremy(1997) 'Consumerism; Greenhouse defects Colombia's flower industry has bloomer into a top dollar earner', *The Guardian*, Manchester, (September 17) p. Society, vol. 4, no.1.

Lewis, Arthur (1955), *The Theory of Economic Growth*, London: Allen & Unwin.

Lochhead, Carolyn (1999) 'Bay Flower Growers Enter Drug War', *San Francisco Chronicle*, (February 26) p.A1:2.

Lucas, Robert (1988), 'On the Mechanics of Economic Development', *Journal of Monetary Economics*, vol. 22, pp. 3-42.

Mendez, Jose (1991), The Development of the Colombian Cut Flower Industry', Working Paper no.660, The World Bank.

Mollenkamp, Carrick (1999), 'Gerald Steven's Bid to Dominate The Retail Floral Industry may Wilt', *Wall Street Journal*, (May 19) p. S2.

Rivera-Batiz, Luis, and Paul Romer (1991a), 'Economic Integration and Endogenous Growth', *The Quarterly Journal of Economics*, vol. 106, pp. 531-55.

Rivera-Batiz, Luis and Paul Romer (1991b), 'International Trade with Endogenous Technological Change', NBER working paper no. 3594.

Roberts, Mark and James Tybout (1997), 'The Decision to Export in Colombia: An Empirical Model of Entry with Sunk Costs', *American Economic Review* , vol. 87, no.4, pp. 545-64.

Rohter, Larry (1999) 'Foreign Presence in Colombia's Flower gardens'. *New York Times*, (May 8) p.1.

Romer, Paul (1990), 'Human Capital and Growth: Theory and Evidence', *Carnegie-Rochester Conference Series on Public Policy*, vol. 32, pp. 251-286.

Romer, Paul (1991), 'Increasing Returns and New Developments in the Theory of Growth', in: William Barnett, et al. Eds., *Equilibrium Theory and Applications, Proceedings of the Sixth International Symposium in Economic Theory and Econometrics*, International Symposia in Economic Theory and Econometrics series, Cambridge University Press: New York.

Romer, Paul (1992), 'Endogenous Technological Change', in: Kevin Hoover, ed., *The New Classical Macroeconomics*, vol.3. International Library of Critical Writings in Economics, vol. 19, Elgar: Aldershot, U.K., distributed in the U.S. by Ashgate:Brookfield, VT.

Thomas, Vinod (1985), 'Linking Macroeconomic and Agricultural Policies for Adjustment with Growth: The Colombian Experience', A World Bank Publication, Baltimore: The John Hopkins University Press.

United Nations *International Trade Statistics Yearbook*, various years.

Wren, C. (1997) 'U.S. Sours on Flowers From Andes', *New York Times*, (February 17) p.8.

Appendix

Since the growth rate can not be solved for explicitly, to solve for the effects of changes in the tariffs and subsidies on growth rates it is necessary to totally differentiate the equation (A1) identifying the equilibrium growth rate. Substituting equation (12) and the law of motion for knowledge into equation (14) yields equation A1:

$$-\alpha\beta H_1 = (\delta - \beta H_1) - \beta A\left[\frac{(1+\pi^2)\frac{\partial V}{\partial A} + (1+\pi^1)\frac{\partial F}{\partial A}}{(1+\pi^2)\frac{\partial V}{\partial H_2} - (1+\pi^1)\frac{\partial F}{\partial H_1}}\right]$$

Totally differentiating equation (A1) and solving for the effect of a change in π^1 on the long run growth rate yields equation A2:

$$\frac{\partial g^*}{\partial \pi^1} = \frac{-\beta\frac{A}{Z}\left(\frac{\partial F}{\partial A}\right) \; -\beta A\frac{(1+\pi^1)}{Z^2}\left(\frac{\partial F}{\partial A}\right)\left(\frac{\partial F}{\partial H_1}\right) \; -\beta A\frac{(1+\pi^2)}{Z^2}\left(\frac{\partial V}{\partial A}\right)\left(\frac{\partial F}{\partial H_1}\right)}{D_1 + D_2}$$

where

$$D_1 = \beta - \alpha\beta + \beta\frac{A}{Z}\left[(1+\pi^1)\frac{\left(\frac{\partial F}{\partial A}\right)}{\partial H_1} + (1+\pi^2)\frac{\left(\frac{\partial V}{\partial A}\right)}{\partial H_1}\right]$$

$$D_2 = \beta\frac{A}{Z^2}\left[(1+\pi^2)\left(\frac{\partial V}{\partial A}\right) + (1+\pi^1)\left(\frac{\partial F}{\partial A}\right)\right]\left[(1+\pi^2)\frac{\left(\frac{\partial V}{\partial H_2}\right)}{\partial H_1} + (1+\pi^1)\frac{\left(\frac{\partial F}{\partial H_1}\right)}{\partial H_1}\right]$$

$$Z = (1+\pi^2)\left(\frac{\partial V}{\partial H_2}\right) - (1+\pi^1)\left(\frac{\partial F}{\partial H_1}\right)$$

Equation (A2) reveals that an increase in the subsidy to export sector one will lead to a positive increase in the long run growth rate. The derivative of the long run growth rate with respect to the subsidy in export sector one is positive. The only term with an ambiguous sign is the equation for (Z). Regardless of whether the equation for (Z) is positive or negative the entire derivative will be positive.

Equation (A3) reveals that an increase in subsidies to export sector two will have a negative effect on long run growth rates:

$$\frac{\partial g^*}{\partial \pi^2} = \frac{-\beta\frac{A}{Z}\left(\frac{\partial V}{\partial A}\right) + \beta A\frac{(1+\pi^1)}{Z^2}\left(\frac{\partial F}{\partial A}\right)\left(\frac{\partial V}{\partial H_2}\right) + \beta A\frac{(1+\pi^2)^2}{Z^2}\left(\frac{\partial V}{\partial A}\right)\frac{\left(\frac{\partial V}{\partial H_2}\right)}{\partial H_1}}{D_1 + D_2}$$

where

$$D_1 = \beta - \alpha\beta + \beta\frac{A}{Z}\left[(1+\pi^1)\frac{\left(\frac{\partial F}{\partial A}\right)}{\partial H_1} + (1+\pi^2)\frac{\left(\frac{\partial V}{\partial A}\right)}{\partial H_1}\right]$$

$$D_2 = \beta\frac{A}{Z^2}\left[(1+\pi^2)\left(\frac{\partial V}{\partial A}\right) + (1+\pi^1)\left(\frac{\partial F}{\partial A}\right)\right]\left[(1+\pi^2)\frac{\left(\frac{\partial V}{\partial H_2}\right)}{\partial H_1} + (1+\pi^1)\frac{\left(\frac{\partial F}{\partial H_1}\right)}{\partial H_1}\right]$$

Once again the only ambiguous term in the derivative of the long run growth rate with respect to a subsidy in export sector two is the equation for (Z). However, examining both cases for (Z) still reveals that the derivative will be negative.

Equation (A4) illustrates that an increase in the tariff in the import competing sector will also have a negative effect on long run growth rates:

$$\frac{\partial g^*}{\partial \pi^m} = \frac{-\beta\frac{A}{Y}\left(\frac{\partial V}{\partial A}\right) + \beta A\frac{(1+\pi^1)}{Y^2}\left(\frac{\partial F}{\partial A}\right)\left(\frac{\partial M}{\partial H_1}\right) + \beta A(1+\pi^m)\frac{(1+\pi_2)}{Y^2}\left(\frac{\partial V}{\partial A}\right)\frac{\left(\frac{\partial M}{\partial H_1}\right)}{\partial H_1}}{D_1 + D_2}$$

where

$$D_1 = \beta - \alpha\beta + \beta\frac{A}{Y}\left[(1+\pi^1)\frac{\left(\frac{\partial F}{\partial A}\right)}{\partial H_1} + (1+\pi^2)\frac{\left(\frac{\partial V}{\partial A}\right)}{\partial H_1}\right]$$

$$D_2 = \beta\frac{A}{Y^2}\left[(1+\pi^2)\left(\frac{\partial V}{\partial A}\right) + (1+\pi^1)\left(\frac{\partial F}{\partial A}\right)\right]\left[(1+\pi^m)\frac{\left(\frac{\partial M}{\partial H_1}\right)}{\partial H_1} + (1+\pi^1)\frac{\left(\frac{\partial F}{\partial H_1}\right)}{\partial H_1}\right]$$

$$Y = -(1+\pi^m)\left(\frac{\partial M}{\partial H_1}\right) - (1+\pi^1)\left(\frac{\partial F}{\partial H_1}\right)$$

In this case, the equation for (Y) is the only term with an ambiguous sign. If the equation for (Y) is positive then the derivative is unambiguously negative. If the equation for (Y) is negative, the derivative will still be negative, even though, the first term in the numerator will be positive and the last term in D_1 will be negative.

9 Prospects for Intra-Latin Integration

In Woody Allen's 1969 film 'Don't Drink the Water', hapless diplomat Axel McGee is given one last chance at success in the Foreign Service, working for his father the Ambassador at an undesirable posting in communist Eastern Europe. In order to establish Axel's character as an incompetent dolt, the audience is told at the outset that while posted in Brazil, he messed up so badly that 'he had the Brazilians *importing coffee!*'. No prior knowledge of trade theory is assumed on the part of the audience; the joke works immediately because everyone knows that Brazilians are supposed to export coffee. For the Brazilians to import coffee is like carrying the proverbial coals to Newcastle. Trade is supposed to move commodities from where they are abundant to where they are scarce - a seeming no-brainer.

On some accounts, Latin America is a collection of Newcastles, all full of coal, and so regional integration is unlikely to be profitable. Michael Michaely (1996) argued that preferential trade agreements in Latin America and the Caribbean would be less successful than similar agreements among European or East Asian countries, and that Latin American countries would be better off seeking integration with the United States. Michaely calculates a trade complementarity index for Latin American country pairs, as well as for the EU, NAFTA, and several current and hypothetical regional trade groupings in Latin America. The index takes a value of 1 when the composition of country j's exports exactly matches the composition of country k's imports (maximum complementarity) and a value of 0 when the set of goods country j exports are not imported at all in country k.[1] Obtaining relatively high trade complementarity scores for the EU and NAFTA, and relatively low scores for MERCOSUR and other possible intra-Latin integration schemes, Michaely concludes that the gains from intra-Latin trade must be limited. Trade complementarity is in some ways similar to the concept of export similarity we have exploited in this book; when export similarity is high, as for example between two coffee producers or two oil producers, trade complementarity is likely to be low. The tempting conclusion is that because the scope for Heckscher-Ohlin-type trade is limited, the gains from liberalization overall must be limited.

Yeats (1997) makes a similar argument with respect to MERCOSUR. He points out that the most rapidly growing commodities in MERCOSUR's internal trade have been capital-intensive goods such as transport equipment and machinery. In 1994, about 63 percent of intra-MERCOSUR exports consisted of manufactures, as compared to 48 percent of MERCOSUR's exports to the world. Since the countries in the MERCOSUR grouping tend to export relatively more agricultural products outside the grouping and relatively more manufactured exports within the grouping, and since data on factor endowments do not seem to suggest a comparative advantage in manufactures, the above type of evidence can be taken as being at least consistent with trade diversion caused by intragroup liberalization, and thus possibly with welfare losses for the countries involved. Again, the problem is perceived to be that regional integration cannot operate effectively on agriculturalor mineral trade, since countries produce products which substitute for each other, and thus that trade in manufactures spurred by intra-Latin integration could be inefficient.

We are now in a position to reassess some of these arguments in light of the empirical work in the preceding chapters. We have shown that there is a long-run trend toward export diversification in Latin America, that it persists to a greater or lesser degree among all Latin American countries, and that diversification continues apace whether countries pursue inward- or outward-looking policies. Indeed, the only force that appears to disrupt the long-toward trend towards diversification is a favorable price shock affecting a country's principal export commodity, as for Colombian coffee and Mexican oil in the late 1970s.

Concomitantly, we learned that measured export similarity between Latin American countries is increasing over time. Recall that we decomposed the progress of export similarity into intra-cluster and intercluster components. Coffee producers have become less like other coffee producers, oil producers less like other oil producers, mining countries less like other mining countries, over time. The measured increase in similarity is due to a stronger force which outweighs intracluster divergence, namely that coffee producers look more like oil producers, which look more like mining countries, and so on. This convergence is due partly to the rise of new manufactured commodities in the region, and partly to the introduction of new 'non-traditional' lines of agricultural products in a number of countries.

Given both the trend towards increasing export diversification and the trend toward intercluster similarity in Latin American exports, it is apparent that export complementarity is likely to be increasing as well. In Michaely's analysis, a high degree of complementarity exists among EU exports, or NAFTA exports, precisely because countries are exporting bundles of manufactured goods in exchange for bundles of imported manufactures which are similar (or look similar at a high degree of aggregation). If this type of Helpman/Krugman trade is indeed what makes for a successful integration agreement, the trend is for such trade to increase in Latin America in the long run. Indeed, the trend toward export similarity between country pairs is driven by the trend toward export diversification by single countries, and we have seen that the trend toward diversification is very strong and persistent.

The above argument does not suffice to overcome the Yeats objection, that intragroup increases in manufactured trade by countries which export agricultural goods extragroup may be evidence of inefficient trade diversion. In the first place, it should be pointed out that not all trade diversion reduces welfare. Even if country A buys from a trade group member with higher production costs rather than an outsider with lower production costs, the motivation for doing so (namely, that no tariff is charged on imports from the group member) means that consumers in country A pay lower prices from which they indeed benefit. The benefits from such lower consumer prices can potentially outweigh the inefficiencies arising from a misallocation of production (Meade, 1955).

Moreover, the manufactures increasingly traded within Latin America may represent true gains from trade based on product differentiation. One would expect that in the international division of labor in the production of differentiated manufactures, Latin American countries would at least produce some varieties consistent with their economic size. A disproportionate focus of intra-Latin trade on these varieties could have several rational economic explanations. First, information asymmetries may cause firms in the region to purchase more heavily from other firms in the region even when the products traded are very similar to comparable non-Latin products. Recall that in the appendix to Chapter Three, we found that Latin American trade is reasonably well explained by standard measures of information cost such as physical distance, the presence or absence of a common border, and linguistic similarity. Thus, on informational grounds alone intra-Latin exports may be preferred.

A second reasonable hypothesis on the emergence of intra-Latin trade in manufactures can be derived from the representative demand theory of Linder (1961). On the Linder hypothesis, countries differ in their composition of demand according to income levels, tastes, and other factors. Because a large share of production is destined for domestic markets to meet this representative demand, production of commodities which are important in a country's consumption becomes more efficient and experiences demand-driven technological change (Schmookler, 1966); in turn, the country then becomes an exporter of these products. While formal models of product differentiation often assume either a uniform distribution of product attributes or a uniform distribution of consumer tastes, a model of demand-driven differentiation suggests that varieties of manufactures produced in one Latin American nation may be in relatively greater demand in other Latin American nations (for example, equipment which embodies capital-saving innovations, or consumer goods which are appropriate for tropical or subtropical conditions).

A lowering of tariff and non-tariff barriers in manufacturing could stimulate intra-Latin trade on either of the above motivations, if the previous trade barriers were sufficiently high *ex ante* to outweigh such motivations. But the stimulus to trade assumes that the barriers are indeed lowered. This brings up a very natural candidate for the observed pattern of intra-Latin trade expansion: the timing of the liberalization itself. MERCOSUR, in particular, has proceeded first on manufacturing liberalization, permitting longer phaseouts for agriculture both for intra-MERCOSUR tariff reduction and for implementation of the common external tariff. Such a pattern is not peculiar to Latin America: many other liberalization schemes (e.g. NAFTA, or the Europe Agreements between the EU and Eastern European countries) have done the same.

The presence of slow phaseouts in agriculture means that potential increases in intra-Latin agricultural trade are in fact suppressed by a continuation of former protectionist policies. This, in turn, happens because there are important efficiency differences in agricultural production between one country and another, leading to political sensitivity to agricultural imports in the less efficient countries. One agricultural commodity which has enjoyed intra-MERCOSUR liberalization is wheat; in late 1966, a surge of imports from Argentina reduced the Brazilian price of wheat from about \$160 per metric ton to a range of \$120-\$140 per metric ton, leading to calls for import quotas by Brazilian producers' organizations (*Journal of Commerce,* 1996). Negotiations over MERCOSUR association agreements for Bolivia, Chile, and Peru each were held up over agricultural sensitivities. If intra-regional differences in agricultural efficiency are substantial, benefits to consumers from intra-Latin agricultural trade may also be substantial; yet the presence of such benefits is not captured by an analysis based on trade complementarity or export similarity.

Moreover, the results of the gravity model we estimated in the appendix to Chapter Three directly falsify the idea that for Latin America, trade complementarity (or export dissimilarity) is important in stimulating trade. If anything, there has been more trade between Latin American countries with similar export portfolios, both before and after the current wave of regional liberalization agreements. We are thus left with two conclusions. First, the fact that many Latin American economies share a similar bundle of agricultural exports is not an important barrier to trade expansion. Second, if such similarity were a problem, it is likely to become less so over time. All Latin American countries are undergoing secular diversification, and the current increase in export similarity is due partially to a rise in differentiated manufactured exports and partially to agricultural diversification country-by-country.

We have found, other things being equal, that more diversified Latin American countries grow faster (Chapter Seven), and that larger Latin American economies are more likely to engage in trade with each other (in the appendix to Chapter Three, the elasticity of both exports and imports with respect to GDP exceeds 1 substantially). Thus, Latin American exports are growing rapidly and becoming steadily more diversified, and such diversification is associated with significant economic growth. Whatever the mechanism of the diversification-growth linkage, whether it comes about through risk reduction, Schumpeterian innovation of exporters, or something else, we know that growth further stimulates trade disproportionately, and that additional trade is likely to be increasingly diversified. This suggests that a virtuous circle linking diversification, growth, and trade is in place.

Finally, we have shown that the return to capital (both domestically financed and foreign direct investment) has historically been relatively high in Latin America as compared to other countries. Consistent with this, there has been more rapid convergence between poor and rich countries in Latin America than in other developing regions. This also suggests optimism regarding the region's prospects. At the time of writing (November 1998), Brazil and the IMF have just completed a new financing agreement, spurred largely by concern that investor overreaction to financial crises in East Asia and Russia could lead to capital flight. Latin American domestic savings rates have been chronically low by world standards, and the region has required steady infusions of both portfolio and direct-investment capital in order to finance capital accumulation (Edwards, 1995). While these inflows of capital have been intermittently interrupted by volatility in international financial markets, our results suggest that in the long run they should persist, and the capital accumulation necessary to finance the growth component of the diversification-growth-trade virtuous circle should be forthcoming.

In conclusion, an appropriate set of stylized facts for Latin American trade includes a long-run trend toward export diversification for most countries, increasing trade of differentiated manufactures among the largest countries, the historical unimportance of complementarity in explaining intra-Latin trade flows, the experience that more diversified Latin American countries have *ceteris paribus* grown more rapidly, and the relatively rapid convergence of Latin American incomes across countries. These facts, taken together, suggest that intra-Latin trade in the future is likely to increasingly resemble the trade in differentiated products observed among the wealthier developed countries. The expansion of such trade is consistent with the achievement of higher levels of economic development. Estimates of the gains from, say, MERCOSUR or the FTAA which are predicated on Heckscher-Ohlin specialization only are likely to be understated. Nonetheless, the ongoing role of the most traditional Latin exports in financing the capital accumulation necessary to sustain this growth is likely to persist.

Note

1. Formally, Michaely defines trade complementarity between countries j and k as

$$C_{jk} = 1 - (\Sigma \, |m_{ik} \;\; x_{ij}|)/2$$

where I indexes commodities, x_{ij} represents the share of commodity I in the exports of country j, and m_{ij} represents the share of commodity I in the imports of country k.

References

Edwards, Sebastian (1995), 'Why Are Savings Rates So Different Across Countries? An International Comparative Analysis', *NBER Working Paper* 5097 (April), Cambridge, Mass:National Bureau of Economic Research.

Linder, Steffan Burestam (1961), *An Essay on Trade and Transformation*, Uppsala: Almqvist and Wiksells.

Meade, James E. (1955), *The Theory of Customs Unions*, Amsterdam: North-Holland.

Michaely, Michael (1996), 'Trade Preferential Agreements in Latin America: An Ex Ante Assessment', *World Bank Policy Research Working Paper* 1583 (March), Washington, DC:World Bank.

Schmookler, Jacob (1966), *Invention and Economic Growth,* Cambridge, Mass.: Harvard University Press.

Yeats, Alexander (1997), 'Does Mercosur's Trade Performance Raise Concerns about the Effects of Regional Trade Agreements?', *World Bank Policy Research Working Paper* 1729 (February), Washington, DC: World Bank.

Bibliography

Adelman, Irma (1995), 'Beyond Export-Led Growth', in Adelman, I. (Ed), *Institutions and Development Strategies: The Selected Essays of Irma Adelman*, Volume I, Edward Elgar, Brookfield, Vermont, pp.290-302.

Adelman, Irma, Bourniaux, Jean-Marc and Waelbroeck, Jean (1995), 'Agricultural Development-led Industrialisation in a Global Perspective', in Adelman, I. (Ed), *Institutions and Development Strategies: The Selected Essays of Irma Adelman*, Volume I, Edward Elgar, Brookfield, Vermont, pp.303-322.

Aitken, Brian, Hanson, Gordon and Harrison, Ann (1997), 'Spillovers, Foreign Investment, and Export Behavior', *Journal of International Economics*, vol. 43, pp. 103-132.

Alam, Asad and Sarath Rajapatirana (1993), 'Trade Reform in Latin America and the Caribbean', *Finance and Development*, vol. 30, no.3.

Allen, Loring (1993), *Venezuelan Economic Development; A Politico-Economic Analysis,* Greenwich, Connecticut: JAI Press.

Amin, Samir (1977), *Imperialism and Unequal Development*, Hassocks: Harvester Press.

Amin Gutiérrez de Piñeres, Sheila (1999), 'Externalities in the Agricultural Export Sector and Economic Growth: A Developing Country Perspective', *Agricultural Economics* , vol. 21, pp. 257-267.

Amin Gutiérrez de Piñeres, Sheila (1996), 'Externalities in the Export Sector and Long Run Growth Rates', *Singapore Economic Review*, vol. 41, no. 1 (April), pp. 13-24.

Amin Gutiérrez de Piñeres, Sheila, and Michael J. Ferrantino (forthcoming), 'The Commodity Composition of Export Portfolios: A Comparative Analysis of Latin America', *Latin American Business Review.*

Amin Gutiérrez de Piñeres, Sheila, and Michael J. Ferrantino (1997), 'Export Diversification and Structural Change: Some Comparisons for Latin America', *The International Executive*, vol. 39 no. 4 (July/August), pp. 465-477.

Amin Gutiérrez de Piñeres, Sheila, and Michael J. Ferrantino (1997), 'Export Diversification and Structural Dynamics in the Growth Process: The Case of Chile', *Journal of Development Economics*, Vol. 52 No. 2, April, pp. 375-391.

Amin Gutiérrez de Piñeres, Sheila, and Michael J. Ferrantino (1999),'Export Sector Dynamics and Economic Growth: The Case of Colombia', *Review of Development Economics*, *October 1999,* vol. 3, no.3, pp. 268-280.

ASOCOLFLORES, various data bases, Bogota, Colombia.

Bahmani-Oskooee, Mohsen and Janardhanan Alse (1993), 'Export Growth and Economic Growth: An Application of Cointegration and Error Correction Modeling', *Journal of Developing Areas*, vol. 27 (July), pp.535-542.

Bahmani-Oskooee, Moshen, Mohtadi Hamid and Shabsign Ghiath (1991), 'Exports, Growth and Causality in LDCS: A Re-examination', *Journal of Development Economics*, vol.36, no.2, pp. 405-415.

Balassa, Bela (1978), 'Exports and Economic Growth: Further Evidence', *Journal of Development Economics*, vol. 5, no. 2, pp. 181-89.

Balassa, Bela (1966), 'Tariff Reductions and Trade in Manufactures', *American Economic Review,* vol. 56, pp. 466-473.

Balasubramanyam, V.N., M.A. Salisu and David Sapsford (1996), 'Foreign Direct Investment and Growth in EP and IS Countries', *The Economic Journal*, Vol. 106, pp. 92-105.

Barro, Robert J. and Xavier Sala-I-Martin (1995), *Economic Growth,* New York: McGraw-Hill.

Behrman, Jere (1976), *Foreign Trade Regimes and Economic Development: Chile,* New York: National Bureau of Economic Research.

Bhagwati, Jagdish (1966), *The Economics of Underdeveloped Countries,* New York: McGraw-Hill.

Bhagwati, Jagdish and T.N. Srinivasan (1975), *Foreign Trade Regimes and Economic Development: India,* New York and London: Columbia University Press for the National Bureau of Economic Research.

Bloomberg News (1998), 'Dole Adds to Its Floral Arrangement', *The Los Angeles Times*, August 5, pp. 2.

Boue, Juan Carlos (1993), *Venezuela: The Political Economy of Oil,* Oxford: Oxford University Press.

Cardoso, Eliana, and Ann Helwege (1992), *Latin America's Economy: Diversity, Trends, and Conflicts,* Cambridge, MA: MIT Press.

Carrada-Bravo, Francisco (1982), *Oil, Money, and the Mexican Economy; A Macroeconomic Analysis,* Boulder, Colorado: Westview Press.

Chua, Hak B. (1993), 'Regional Spillovers and Economic Growth', *Yale University Economic Growth Center Discussion Paper*, no. 700 (September), New Haven: Yale University.

Chen, Tain-jy and Tang, Depiao (1987), 'Comparing Technical Efficiency Between Import-Substitution- Oriented and Export-Oriented Foreign Firms in a Developing Economy', *Journal of Development Economics*, vol. 26, pp. 277-289.

Chenery, Hollis, Ahluwalia, Montek, Bell, C.L.G., Duloy, J. and Jolly, R. (1974), *Redistribution with Growth,* Oxford, England: Oxford University Press.

Chenery, Hollis and Syrquin Moshe (1975), *Patterns of Development 1950-1970*, Oxford University Press: London.

Clerides, Sofronis, Saul, Lach and James Tybout (1998), 'Is Learning by Exporting Important? Micro- Dynamic Evidence from Colombia, Mexico and Morocco', *Quarterly Journal of Economics*, vol. 113, no.3, pp. 903-47.

Cohen, Alvin and Frank Gunter, Eds. (1992), *The Colombian Economy: Issues of Trade and Development*, Boulder: Westview Press.

Colombia Today (1990), 'Colombian Export Diversification. Colombia Information Service', vol.24, No.12.

Dean, Judith, Desai, Seema and James Riedel (1994), 'Trade Policy Reform in Developing Countries Since 1985: A Review of the Evidence', *World Bank Discussion Paper 267*, Washington, DC: World Bank.

De Gregorio, Jose (1992), 'Economic Growth in Latin America', *Journal of Development Economics*, vol. 39, pp.59-84.

Dessus, Sebastien (1999), 'Total Factor Productivity and Outward Orientation in Taiwan: What is the Nature of the Relationship', in Fu,T., Huang, C. and Lovell, A. (Eds), *Economic Efficiency and Productivity Growth in the Asia Pacific Region*, Edward Elgar: Brookfield, Vermont.

Deveny, Kathleen (1985), 'Now The Flower Business Is Blooming All Year', *Business Week*, (December 23) vol. 2926, pp. 59.

Devlin, Robert (1996), 'In Defense of Mercosur', *The IDB* (December 3), Washington, DC: Inter-American Development Bank.

Dixit, Avinash and Victor D. Norman (1980), *Theory of International Trade*, Cambridge: Cambridge University Press.

Dollar, David (1986), 'Technological Innovation, Capital Mobility and the Product Cycle in North-South Trade', *American Economic Review*, vol 76, no. 1, pp. 177-190.

Easterlin, Richard A. (1996), *Growth Triumphant: The Twenty-First Century in Historical Perspective,* Ann Arbor: University of Michigan Press.

The Economist (1993). 'Colombian business-Fallow ground', (October 23) vol. 329, Issue 7834, p. 86.

Edwards, Sebastian (1993), 'Openness, Trade Liberalization, and Growth in Developing Countries', *Journal of Economic Literature*, vol. 31, pp. 1358-1393.

Edwards, Sebastian (1995), 'Why Are Savings Rates So Different Across Countries? An International Comparative Analysis', *NBER Working Paper* 5097 (April). Cambridge, Mass: National Bureau of Economic Research.

Edwards, S. and A. Edwards (1987), *Monetarism and Liberalization: The Chilean Experiment*. Cambridge, Mass: Ballinger.

El Maliaakah, Ragaei, Oystein Noreng and Barry W. Poulson (1984), *Petroleum and Economic Development,* Lexington, Massachusetts: Lexington Books.

Elias, Victor (1985), 'Government Expenditures on Agriculture and Agricultural Growth in Latin America', International Food Policy Research Institute Research Report no. 50.

Emery, Robert (1967), 'The Relation of Exports and Economic Growth', *Kyklos*, vol.20, no.4, pp.470 84.

Esfahani, Hadi (1991), 'Exports, Imports, and Economic Growth in Semi-industrialized Countries', *Journal of Development Economics*, vol. 35, no.1, pp. 93-116.

Ethier, Wilfred (1982), 'National and International Returns to Scale in the Modern

Theory of International Trade', *American Economic Review* ,vol. 72 (June), pp. 950-959.

Finger, J. Michael and Mordecai E. Kreinin (1979), 'A Measure of "Export Similarity" and Its Possible Uses', *Economic Journal*, vol. 89, pp. 905-12.

Foxley, Alejandro (1983), *Latin American Experiments in Neo-Conservative Economics*, Berkeley: University of California Press.

Frank, Charles, and Richard Webb, Eds. (1977), *Income Distribution: Policy Alternatives in Developing Countries,* Washington, D.C. Brookings Institution.

Furtado, Celso (1976), *Economic Development of Latin America: Historical Background and Contemporary Problems*, 2nd edition, Cambridge: Cambridge University Press.

Gagnon, Joseph E. and Andrew K. Rose (1995), 'Dynamic Persistence of Industry Trade Balances: How Pervasive is the Product Cycle?', *Oxford Economic Papers* vol. 47, no. 2, pp. 29-248.

Garcia Garcia, Jorge and Gabriel Montes Llamas (1988), *Coffee Boom, Government Expenditure, and Agricultural Prices: the Colombian Experience*, Research Report no.68, Washington, D.C.: International Food Policy Research Institute.

Grilli, Enzo and Maw Cheng Yang (1988), 'Primary Commodity Prices, Manufactured Goods Prices, and Terms of Trade of Developing Countries: What the Long Run Shows', *World Bank Economic Review*, vol. 2, no. 1.

Grossman, Gene and Elhanan Helpman (1990), 'Comparative Advantage and Long Run Growth', *American Economic Review*, vol. 80, pp. 796-815.

Grossman, Gene and Elhanan Helpman (1991), 'Endogenous Product Cycles', *Economic Journal*, vol.101, pp. 1214-1229.

Grossman, Gene and Elhanan Helpman (1991), *Innovation and Growth in the Global Economy*, Cambridge, MA: MIT Press.

Grubel, Herbert G. and Peter Lloyd (1975), *Intra-Industry Trade: The Theory and Measurement of International Trade in Differentiated Products*, New York: John Wiley.

Hallberg, Kristin (1991), *Colombia: Industrial Competition and Performance*, Washington, D.C.: The World Bank.

Hardenburg, R., Watada, A. and Wang, C. (1990), 'The Commercial Storage of Fruits, Vegetables, and Florist and Nursery Stocks', U.S. Department of Agriculture: Agriculture Handbook Number 66.

Helleiner, Gerald (1986), 'Outward Orientation, Import Instability and African Economic Growth: An Empirical Investigation', in Sanjaya Lall and Frances Stewart, eds., *Theory and Reality in Economic Development*, London: Macmillan.

Helpman, Elhanan (1981), 'International Trade in the Presence of Product Differentiation, Economies of Scale, and Monopolistic Competition: A Chamberlin-Heckscher-Ohlin Approach', *Journal of International Economics*, vol. 11 (August), pp. 305-340.

Helpman, Elhanan and Paul Krugman (1985), *Market Structure and Foreign Trade.* Cambridge, Mass: MIT Press.

Hogg, Robert V. and Elliot A. Tanis (1977), *Probability and Statistical Inference*, New York: Macmillan.

Hutchison, Michael and Nirvikar Singh (1992), 'Exports, Non Exports and Externalities: a Granger Causality Approach', *International Economic Journal*, vol.6, no.2, pp. 79-94.

Inter-American Development Bank (1998), *Integration and Trade in the Americas.* Department of Integration and Regional Programs; Division of Integration, Trade, and Hemispheric Analysis; Statistics and Quantitative Analysis Unit, Periodic Note (August), Washington, DC: IADB.

International Monetary Fund, *International Financial Statistics Yearbook*, various years.

Islam, Nazrul (1995), 'Growth Empirics: A Panel Data Approach', *Quarterly Journal of Economics*, vol. 110, No. 4 (November), pp. 1127-1170.

Jung, Woo and Peyton Marshall (1985), 'Exports, Growth and Causality in Developing Countries', *Journal of Development Economics*, vol.18, no.2, pp. 1-12.

Katrak, Homi (1989), 'Imported Technologies and R&D in a Newly Industrializing Country: The Experience of Indian Enterprises', *Journal of Development Economics*, vol. 31, pp. 123-139.

Kellman, Mitchell and Tim Schroeder (1983), 'The Export Similarity Index: Some Structural Tests', *Economic Journal*, vol. 93, pp. 193-8.

Keynes, John Maynard (1938), 'The Policy of Government Storage of Foodstuffs and Raw Materials', *Economic Journal*, vol. 48, September, pp. 449-60.

Kose, M. Ayhan (1998), 'Explaining Business Cycles in Small Open Economies: How Much Do World Prices Matter?', Brandeis University, processed.

Kravetz, Stacy (1998), 'Retailing: King of Pineapples Tiptoes to Tulips for Faster Growth', *Wall Street Journal,* (July 6) p. A17.

Kravis, Irving (1970), 'Trade as a Handmaiden of Growth', *Economic Journal*, vol. 80, no. 320, pp. 850-72.

Krueger, Anne (1978), *Foreign Trade Regimes and Economic Development: Liberalization Attempts and Consequences*, Cambridge, MA: Ballinger Pub. Co. for NBER.

Krugman, Paul (1979), 'Increasing Returns, Monopolistic Competition, and International Trade', *Journal of International Economics*, vol. 9, pp. 469-479.

Krugman, Paul (1979), 'A Model of Innovation, Technology Transfer and the World Distribution of Income', *Journal of Political Economy,* vol. 87, pp. 253-266.

Krugman, Paul (1981), 'Intraindustry Specialization and the Gains from Trade', *Journal of Political Economy,* vol. 89, pp. 959-973.

Lal,D. and Rajapatirana, S. (1987), 'Foreign Trade Regimes and Economic Growth in Developing Countries', *World Bank Research Observer* , vol 2, pp. 189-218.

Lennard, Jeremy(1997) 'Consumerism; Greenhouse defects Colombia's flower industry has bloomer into a top dollar earner', *The Guardian*, Manchester, (September 17) p. Society, vol. 4, no.1.

Levine, Daniel (1989), 'Venezuela: The Nature, Sources and Prospects of Democracy', in *Democracy in Developing Countries: Latin America* edited by Larry Diamond, Juan J. Linz and Seymour Martin Lipset, Boulder, Co: Lynne Rienner Publishers.

Levine, Ross, and David Renelt (1992), 'A Sensitivity Analysis of Cross-Country Growth Regressions', *American Economic Review*, vol. 82, no. 4 (September), pp. 942-963.

Lewis, Arthur (1955), *The Theory of Economic Growth*, London: Allen & Unwin.

Lieuwen, Edwin (1954), *Petroleum in Venezuela; A History*, New York: Russell & Russell.

Lochhead, Carolyn (1999) 'Bay Flower Growers Enter Drug War', *San Francisco Chronicle*, (February 26) p.A1:2.

Lord, Montague and Greta Boye (1991), 'The Determinants of International Trade in Latin America's Commodity Exports', in Miguel Urrutia, ed., *Long-Term Trends in Latin American Economic Development*, Baltimore: John Hopkins University Press for the Inter-American Development Bank.

Lucas, Robert (1988), 'On the Mechanics of Economic Development', *Journal of Monetary Economics*, vol. 22, pp. 3-42.

Linder, Steffan Burestam (1961), *An Essay on Trade and Transformation*, Uppsala: Almqvist and Wiksells.

Maddison, Angus (1991), 'Economic and Social Conditions in Latin America, 1913-1950', in Miguel Urrutia, ed., *Long-Term Trends in Latin American Economic Development*, Baltimore: John Hopkins University Press for the Inter-American Development Bank.

Markusen, James (1986), 'Explaining the Volume of Trade', *American Economic Review*, vol. 76, no. 5, pp. 1002-1011.

Markusen, James (1986), 'Explaining the Volume of Trade: An Eclectic Approach', *American Economic Review*, vol. 76, no. 5 (December), pp. 1002-1011.

McCloskey, Donald N. (1985), *The Rhetoric of Economics*, Madison: University of Wisconsin Press.

Meade, James E. (1955), *The Theory of Customs Unions*, Amsterdam: North-Holland.

Mendez, Jose (1991), The Development of the Colombian Cut Flower Industry', Working Paper no.660, The World Bank.

Michaely, M. (1977), 'Exports and Growth: An Empirical Investigation', *Journal of Development Economics*, vol. 4, no. 1. pp. 49-53.

Michaely, Michael (1994), 'Trade-Preferential Agreements in Latin America: An Ex-Ante Assessment', Latin America and the Caribbean Region, World Bank,

Washington, D.C.

Mollenkamp, Carrick (1999), 'Gerald Steven's Bid to Dominate The Retail Floral Industry may Wilt', *Wall Street Journal*, (May 19) p. S2.

Moschos, Demetrios (1989), 'Export Expansion, Growth and the Level of Economic Development', *Journal of Development Economics*, vol. 30, pp. 93-102.

Myint, Hla (1964), *The Economics of the Developing Countries*, New York: Praeger.

Organization of American States (1997), *Trade and Integration Agreements in the Americas: An Analytical Compendium,* Washington, DC: OAS.

Nicholson, Joel, Juan España and Sheila Amin Gutiérrez de Piñeres (1998), 'Government Regulations and FDI: A historical perspective of Mexico', working paper.

Noland, Marcus (1997), 'Has Asian Export Performance Been Unique?', *Journal of International Economics,* vol. 43, no.1/2 (August), pp.79-102.

Ocampo, Jose and L. Villar (1994), 'Colombian Manufactured Exports, 1967-1991' in *Manufacturing for Export in the Developing World: Problems and Possibilities*, Edited by G.K. Helleiner, NY:Routledge.

Pearson, Charles (1994), 'The Asian Export Ladder', in Shu-Chin Yang ed. *Manufactured Exports of East Asian Industrializing Economics*, Amonk: M.E. Sharpe.

Pogany, Peter and William A. Donnelly (1998), 'The Income Elasticity of Trade: Theory, Evidence and Implications', *U.S. International Trade Commission Office of Economics Working Paper* 98-09-A (September 3), Washington, DC: USITC.

Prebisch, Raul (1950), *The Economic Development of Latin America and its Principal Problems*, New York: U.N. Economic Commission on Latin America, United Nations.

Prebisch, Raul (1959), 'International Trade and Payments in an Era of Coexistence Commercial Policy in the Underdeveloped Countries', *American Economic Review*, vol. 49, no. 2, pp.251-273.

Randall, Laura (1987), *The Political Economy of Venezuelan Oil*, New York: Praeger Publishers.

Rivera-Batiz, Luis, and Paul Romer (1991), 'Economic Integration and Endogenous Growth', *The Quarterly Journal of Economics*, vol. 106, pp. 531-55.

Rivera-Batiz, Luis and Paul Romer (1991), 'International Trade with Endogenous Technological Change', NBER working paper no. 3594.

Rivera, Sandra (1995), 'After NAFTA: Western Hemisphere Trade Liberalization and Alternative Paths to Integration', *Social Science Journal*, vol 32, no.4.

Roberts, Mark and James Tybout (1997), 'The Decision to Export in Colombia: An Empirical Model of Entry with Sunk Costs', *American Economic Review*, vol. 87, no.4, pp. 545-64.

Rohter, Larry (1999) 'Foreign Presence in Colombia's Flower gardens', *New York Times*, (May 8) p.1.

Romer, Paul (1990), 'Human Capital and Growth: Theory and Evidence', *Carnegie-Rochester Conference Series on Public Policy*, vol. 32, pp. 251-286.

Romer, Paul (1991), 'Increasing Returns and New Developments in the Theory of Growth', in: William Barnett, et al. eds., *Equilibrium Theory and Applications, Proceedings of the Sixth International Symposium in Economic Theory and Econometrics*, International Symposia in Economic Theory and Econometrics series, Cambridge University Press: New York.

Romer, Paul (1992), 'Endogenous Technological Change', in: Kevin Hoover, ed., *The New Classical Macroeconomics*, vol.3. International Library of Critical Writings in Economics, vol. 19, Elgar: Aldershot, U.K., distributed in the U.S. by Ashgate:Brookfield, VT.

Rosenstein-Rodan, Paul (1943), 'Problems of Industrialization of Eastern and South-Eastern Europe', *The Economic Journal*, vol. 53, pp. 202-211.

Sachs, Jeffery and Andrew Warner (1995), 'Economic Reform and the Process of Global Integration', *Brookings Papers on Economic Activity*, vol. 1, pp. 1-95.

Sachs, Jeffrey and Andrew Warner (1995), 'Economic Reform and the Process of Integration,' *Brookings Papers on Economic Activity*, vol. 1, pp. 1-118.

Sala-I-Martin, Xavier (1997), 'I Just Ran Two Million Regressions', *American Economic Review,* Vol. 87, No. 2 (May), pp. 178-183.

Salazar-Carrillo (1994), *Oil and Development in Venezuela During the Twentieth Century*, Westport, CT: Praeger Publishers.

Schmookler, Jacob (1966), *Invention and Economic Growth*, Cambridge, Mass: Harvard University Press.

Segerstrom, Paul, T. Anant and Elias Dinopolous (1990), 'A Schumpeterian Model of the Product Life Cycle', *American Economic Review*, vol. 80, pp. 1077-1092.

Skidmore, Thomas and Peter H. Smith, (1992), *Modern Latin America*, 3rd edition. New York: Oxford University Press.

Serletis, Apostolos (1992), 'Export Growth and Canadian Economic Development', *Journal of Development Economics*, vol. 38 no. 1, pp.133-45.

Singer, Hans W. (1950), 'The Distribution of Gains Between Investing and Borrowing Countries', *American Economic Review*, vol. 40 (May), pp. 473-85.

Singer, Hans W. (1952), 'The Mechanics of Economic Development', *The Indian Economic Review.*

Singer, Hans W. (1987), 'Terms of Trade and Economic Development', in *The New Palgrave: A Dictionary of Economics*, John Eatwell, Murray Milgate and Peter Newman, eds., London: The Macmillan Press.

Summers, Robert and Alan Heston (1988), 'The Penn World Table (Mark 5): An Expanded Set of International Comparisons', 1950-1988', *Quarterly Journal of Economics*, vol. 106 no. 2, pp. 327-368.

Taylor, Brian (1996), *Global Financial Data*, Alhambra, Ca.

Teichman, Judith (1988), *Policymaking in Mexico*, Boston: Allen & Unwin.

Thomas, Vinod (1985), 'Linking Macroeconomic and Agricultural Policies for

Adjustment with Growth: The Colombian Experience', A World Bank Publication, Baltimore: The John Hopkins University Press.

Thoumi, Francisco (1995), *Political Economy and Illegal Drugs in Colombia*, London: Lynne Rienner Publishers.

United Nations *International Trade Statistics Yearbook*, various years.

Urrutia, Miguel (1991), 'Conclusions' in Miguel Urrutia, ed., *Long-Term Trends in Latin American Economic Development*, Baltimore: John Hopkins University Press for the Inter-American Development Bank.

U.S. International Trade Commission (1997), *The Dynamic Effects of Trade Liberalization: An Empirical Analysis*, publication 3069 (October); Washington, DC: USITC.

Velasco-S, Jesus-Augustin, (1983), *Impacts of Mexican Oil Policy on Economic and Political Development*, Lexington, Mass: Lexington Books.

Vernon, R. (1966), 'International Investment and International Trade in the Product Cycle', *Quarterly Journal of Economics*, vol. 80, pp. 190-207.

Wolf, Martin (1982), *India's Exports*, New York: Oxford University Press for the World Bank.

Worldmark Encyclopedia of the Nations (1984), Detroit, MI: Gale Research, Allen.

Wren, C. (1997) 'U.S. Sours on Flowers From Andes', *New York Times*, (February 17) p.8.

Yaghmaian, Behzad (1994), 'An Empirical Investigation of Exports, Development and Growth in Developing Countries: Challenging the Neoclassical Theory of Export-led Growth' in *World Development*, vol. 22, no.12, pp.1977-1995.

Yeats, Alexander (1997), 'Does Mercosur's Trade Performance Raise Concerns About the Effects of Regional Trade Arrangements?', *World Bank Policy Research Working Paper* No. 1729 (February), Washington, DC: World Bank.

Index